TIK

This is Kenya

LaMoin Cunningham

Faithful Life Publishers
FaithfulLifePublishers.com
888.720.0950

Copyright © 2012 LaMoin Cunningham
ISBN: 978-1-937129-57-6

FOR ADDITIONAL COPIES CONTACT
LaMoin Cunningham
P.O. Box 804
Talbott, TN 37877

Phone: 423-586-0504
Email: LaMoinBill@aol.com

Website: LifeWithLaMoin.com

Published and printed by:
Faithful Life Publishers
3335 Galaxy Way
North Fort Myers, FL   33903

888.720.0950

www.FaithfulLifePublishers.com
info@FLPublishers.com

All rights reserved. No part of this publication may be reproduced, stored in a retrieval system, or transmitted in any form or by any means—electronic, mechanical, photocopy, recording, or any other—without the permission of the author and/or Faithful Life Publishers.

Printed in the United States of America.

18 17 16 15 14 13 12   1 2 3 4 5

Dedication

I want to dedicate this book to my three children: Wyvonna Pacheco, Shaleen Fowler, and Gregory Cunningham. Thank you for your willingness and obedience to follow your dad and me as we followed the Lord. You suffered much, but complained little. I am sorry our mission work brought you a lack of roots, pain, and much hardship. I think God has rewards in heaven for missionary kids. I love you with all of my heart - always and forever.

Introduction

I was brought up in a non-Christian family and was saved at the age of eighteen, after I heard the gospel for the first time. Three months later, I surrendered my life to God. My surrender was full surrender – for life.

I was only twenty-four years old with a toddler, an infant, and three months pregnant with our son when we went to Ethiopia as missionaries. I had to adjust to being a wife, a mother, and a missionary almost at the same time. It was hard. We served God in Ethiopia until civil war and the Communist take-over forced us to leave. We went directly from Africa to Australia.

We had a wonderful but difficult ministry in Australia - until my health broke. I had an emotional breakdown due to many chemical imbalances in my body. It forced us to return to America. We feared I could no longer handle the stresses of the mission field, so Bill took the pastorate of a church in Texas. The recuperation took two years, a lot of prayer, determination, and medical help to bounce back – but I did!

God had not changed his calling on our lives, and we had not retreated from our surrender. We were missionaries. I had recuperated from my physical problems, and God began to burden our hearts about returning to Kenya. My life was still fully surrendered to God, but I did not want to go. It wasn't because I didn't want to continue missionary service or to live in Kenya. But I knew our three teenagers would have to go to boarding school. I rebelled at the idea.

One day as I was struggling, I opened my Bible at random, and my eyes fell on (Isaiah 54:13), "And all thy children shall be taught of the Lord; and great shall be the peace of thy children." Coincidence? No – it was God! He promised me in that verse He would take care of my children, and they would have great peace. At that moment, I surrendered to go to Kenya. I committed my precious children to Him.

Kenya was a beautiful country, and the standard of living was much better than in Ethiopia. I enjoyed our ministry. There were many frustrations and hard times, but those are part of life. Of course we experienced a few more challenges than people have in developed countries. But I love adventure and challenges. We have learned to thrive on chaos, so most of it was interesting and exciting.

I am writing about my personal life in Kenya. Missionaries usually present the ministry. This is not my purpose. Naturally, the ministry was the focus, but missionaries *do* have a personal life – that is my focus in this book.

I loved Kenya, so the things I write about are not intended to discredit the people or the country. My purpose is to portray our personal lives and frustrations in living in an underdeveloped country. I hope you can live with me through the experiences, and you can be entertained for a short time. Please don't judge me as being "unspiritual." God is my judge. I am 100% human flesh, and my spirit is willing, but my flesh is oftentimes weak. I am dedicated to serving God. However, I am not perfect. My soul was saved by the grace of God, but my flesh has not been redeemed. One day it will be changed, but just like the Apostle Paul, I don't always do the things I should, but many times I do the things I should not do – just like you. I am still striving toward the prize of the high calling of God in Christ Jesus – so cut me some slack. Be patient with me – God is still working on me.

Throughout the book, you will notice the letters TIK – This is Kenya. This word was used often as an explanation of difficult circumstances. It always made us laugh. It is important to maintain a sense of humor. Many times we had to strive to see the humor in nerve breaking situations. Laughter is therapeutic, and it will help us to endure many of the problems in this life. In (Proverbs 17:22), the Lord said a merry heart does good like a medicine. When we were frustrated at something the people did - or at the country - we would express it by saying, TIK. No further comment was needed. We understood. Therefore, I felt it was the appropriate title for this book.

My daughter, Shaleen, graciously agreed to write some of her memories. They will be included in the last chapter of this book.

Okay, let's take a trip to Kenya.

Table of Contents

1. Here We Go Again 1
2. Welcome to Kenya 17
3. Tears and Angels 22
4. Frustration, Fun, and Friends 29
5. Our Home in Nairobi 41
6. Plants, Actors, and a Piece of Junk 45
7. They Wrapped Me in Six Yards of Cloth 50
8. Motorcycles, Rain, and Cockroaches 59
9. Collecting Elephant Dung on Mt. Elgon 69
10. A Vacation from Hell 75
11. The Night Train to Mombasa 84
12. They Cut His Throat 87
13. My Key Frustration 93
14. Worms in the Rice 96
15. Me? A Stock Car Driver 100
16. The Nightmare on December 12 104
17. The Shooting Started at Midnight 117
18. Greg Almost Died 124
19. More Surgery for Wyvonna 129
20. A Much Needed Furlough 132
21. A Maniac Mechanic 136
22. A Fat Neck in Utah 147
23. Parting Was Not Sweet Sorrow 151
24. He Stepped on My Last Nerve 160
25. Run Over By a Motor Boat 163
26. Capitol City Baptist Church 175
27. We Rescued the Captive Americans 179
28. My Job at the American Embassy 183
29. Bad News from Home 194
30. A Painful Experience 202
31. Challenges for a Missionary 207
32. Memories from my Daughter, Shaleen 212
About the Author 233

Chapter 1
Here We Go Again

I hate goodbyes! I would rather just sneak away, and not have to go through the agony of the hugs, kisses, and tears. Some people don't try to hold back the tears, but my mother always said, "Don't cry. It makes it harder for the one who is leaving."

I remember saying goodbye to my brother when he was going to Germany as a soldier. I was a teenager, and I loved him dearly. I didn't think I would ever see him again. Mother had cautioned me before getting to the airport, "Don't cry." But, I couldn't help it! I hugged him, watched him get on the plane, saw him wave from the window – and I lost control. I was bawling! My mother's heart was breaking, but she was waving, and through her clinched teeth and set smile she was saying to me, "Don't cry. It will hurt him more."

My mother always waited until we were out of sight, and then she would cry for a half a day.

It was time for us to say goodbye again. We knew, under normal circumstances, we would not see our loved ones again for four years. We were going to Africa! We were also saying goodbye to the country of our birth – the country we *love*. The trip to the airport was much like a trip to a cemetery. When a plane is waiting, you can't tarry too long – and that's good - so we said goodbye to our family. With tears staining our cheeks, we boarded a plane to again take us halfway around the world. We had done this too many times in the past. I hated the tightness in my heart, the lump in my throat that was choking me, and the salty tears which refused to stay in my eyes. But goodbyes are a part of the job description of a missionary.

When anyone says goodbye to loved ones, you never know if you will see them again, but for a missionary the feeling is even worse. We were so far away. If we or a family member got sick, it was difficult to go home. We have experienced surgeries, life threatening accidents, severe illnesses, and deaths of loved ones while on the mission field. We went through it alone, with God's help. It would have been so nice to have loved ones close to give comfort.

When we said goodbye that time, we had a whole different bundle of emotions. We wanted to do the Lord's will, but we knew when we arrived in Kenya, the hardest goodbyes of all were waiting for us. Our children were teenagers, and they were old enough to feel the fear of going to a new country. Sure, there was excitement. But, they knew before long, they would have to leave Mom and Dad and go to live in a boarding school. It would be the first time for them to be away from us for long periods of time. We were all experiencing a multitude of mixed emotions. All of us tried to focus on the trip - and not on the future. (Philippians 1:19) says, "For unto you it is given, in the behalf of Christ, not only to believe on him, but also to suffer for his sake." Many are willing to believe, but few are willing to suffer.

We had so many mixed emotions. We had been traveling across the United States in a motor home for over a year. That might sound exciting – like an extended vacation - but after living in twenty-four feet of space and speaking in hundreds of churches, we were tired. Our kids were good travelers. They had done this all of their lives – but they were tired of being on display. They were tired of well-meaning church members saying, "Say something in African." We were eager to be settled into a home again, but we knew home would never be the same. The kids would have to be away from home for three months, then home for a month.

The prior preparation had also been tiring. Before leaving, we had spent weeks in sorting and packing our crates to ship to Kenya. We take so many things for granted in America – furniture, large and small kitchen appliances, bed linens, dishes, clothing, food items, cleaning supplies, tools, teaching materials - and the list continues. Just take a look around your house. Most of the things you see could not be purchased in Kenya. We had to take those things with us. You might wonder, "Why can't you live like the people there?" Well, for most Americans, it is a bit difficult to adjust to living in a mud hut and sleeping on the ground. To maintain our mental and physical health, we needed some of the comforts our culture provides.

We wanted a few days of fun and relaxation before we had to face the culture shock, family separation, and individual responsibilities which were ahead of us. We decided to visit some other countries on the way to Africa. We could visit missionary friends along the way. Back then the airlines didn't charge us to stop over in different places.

England

We were so tired when we left the States. The many hours in the plane had settled us emotionally, but we were physically exhausted. Our missionary friend met us at the airport in London, and we began our two hour journey to his home in Coventry. Bill was so tired; he quickly went to sleep when we left London. I wondered how he could sleep and possibly miss something exciting. But he said he couldn't hold his eyes open. I was exhausted also, but I was in England! I was going to enjoy every minute and see everything I could. I didn't want to miss anything.

Our friends were so kind and graciously showed us many places of interest. We walked through the city of Coventry and gazed at the life-sized statue of Lady Godiva. She was sitting on a horse, and her long hair covered the upper half of her body. I think this was the first time the love of history was awakened in me. Suddenly, I remembered being awake in my high school history class. (I hated history.) I vaguely remembered hearing about this naughty lady who rode naked through the streets of Coventry to protest the taxes her husband had imposed on the people. Now, there she was in a life sized statue in the center of the town! That was in my history book! Do you remember the story? Do you remember there was also a peeping Tom? All of the people of Coventry had agreed they would not look upon her nakedness during this protest. However, one guy couldn't resist the temptation. He climbed up in a tall building and peeped out the window. We saw the building where he got into trouble for looking at her. Wow! Now I was *seeing* history, and it ignited a flame within me.

This was not my first trip to a foreign country. We had been missionaries for several years, but I can't remember a time before when the love of history had been awakened within me. Maybe I was just coming out of culture shock from the things I had experienced in the other countries! But since then, I have become an avid reader of travel in countries all over the world – and an avid traveler. I have had the privilege of visiting about fifty countries. I thank God for the many experiences He has given me. I have lived a life I would never have thought was possible. There are many perks in serving the Lord!

After a couple of exciting days in Coventry, we rented a car and drove through Northern England to Edinburgh, Scotland. The English countryside was so beautiful with green rolling hills and quaint villages. Some of the cottages were ancient and even had thatched roofs.

Here We Go Again

We were enjoying the beautiful scenery as we traveled along on the "motorway" and tried to stay out of the way of the speeding traffic. Those people drive fast! Bill wasn't paying attention to his speed, and we were totally pre-occupied in looking at all of this gorgeous country. Suddenly we noticed a police car directly behind us - blinking the lights. Bill and I looked at the speedometer. *Oh, no! Is that one hundred miles an hour or kilometers? It was miles!* I felt a hot wave of fear wash over me. *How much trouble are we in? How much do tickets cost in England?*

Bill pulled over into the right lane to prepare to stop, and that "jam sandwich" flew past us like we were sitting still. (At that time, the Brits called the police cars "jam sandwiches," because they were white with a red stripe in the middle – now they have changed to a bright yellow and blue checkerboard pattern.) The policeman just wanted us to get out of his way! Evidently we were going too slowly! It took a couple of minutes for my heart to drop back into its normal position as we traveled on down the motorway.

Scotland

We finally arrived in the large city of Edinburgh. Scotland! I never thought I would visit the land of kilts and bag pipes. We didn't know anyone in Edinburgh, but our friends in Coventry had told us about a bed and breakfast we could check out. We asked a few folks about the B&B, but they couldn't tell us how to get there. Maybe we just didn't understand them. Yes, they spoke English - but not our kind of English. I love the accent, but it makes it difficult to understand them sometimes. We were hungry. We saw a little sandwich and coffee shop, so we decided to get a snack and then use the phone to call the number of the B&B which our friends had given us. After we ate, the kids and I stayed inside the coffee shop, and Bill went outside to a phone booth to make the call. After some time he came back inside. I saw the frustration on his face before he spoke.

"What's wrong?" I asked.

"I can't use that phone."

"What do you mean – you can't use the phone?"

The kids and I were trying not to laugh. He was already angry and frustrated, and we knew our laughter would not help the situation, but we thought it was funny.

"Okay," I said, "let's go out there and try to figure it out."

We all went outside to the phone booth. The kids sat on a bench while I went to the phone booth with Bill. I couldn't understand what could be so hard about making a phone call in an English speaking country. The instructions on the phone were in English.

"It tells you what to do. Lift the receiver, wait for the sound of the pip, pip, then deposit your coin and dial."

"Yeah, I know what it says, but I never did hear the pip, pip," he growled.

"Well, try again."

He tried again and never heard the "pip, pip." I stepped up to the phone with complete confidence – but dreading to make him look bad. I lifted the receiver, and waited for the pip, pip. Were we both deaf, ignorant, even stupid – or what? I never heard the pip, pip either. I couldn't believe it! Then it got funny. Bill never did see the humor in it. This "pip, pip" thing was getting on his nerves. The kids and I couldn't hold our laughter any longer. The more he fumed, the more we laughed – and the more we laughed, the more he fumed.

Finally, a kind looking lady came down the street, and I asked her to please show us how to use the telephone. Now, I must admit, I felt somewhat intimidated and embarrassed by the fact that we spoke English, the instructions were in English, but we couldn't figure it out.

In her pleasant Scottish accent the lady said, "Well, you just lift the receiver, listen until you hear the pip, pip, deposit your coin, and dial your number."

Bill said, "Yeah, I tried that, but I never heard the pip, pip." We finally asked the lady to dial the number for us, which she did. I don't know how she heard the pip, pip but she obviously did, and Bill was able to finally talk to the people at the B&B. They had rooms available, and he made arrangements for us to stay there.

On the way to the B&B, we stopped at a traffic light. Bill revved the engine without paying attention to the man who was crossing the street in front of us. When the man heard the engine, he must have thought Bill was taking off. He whirled around to face us as he began to run. His face looked frozen with terror! He began to run – frightened half to death. I thought Bill had scared him on purpose.

"Bill, you should be ashamed for scaring that man." How can a person be angry and laughing at the same time? I'm not sure, but I accomplished it.

"I didn't do it on purpose. I didn't even notice that he was crossing. I was just revving the engine to make sure that the car didn't stall."

"Yeah, sure, Dad," the kids contributed. They were laughing hysterically – even though they felt sorry for the man, because he was so scared.

The light changed to green, and Bill said, "I'm really sorry I scared that guy. I would like to apologize to him, but I have to keep moving with the traffic."

Soon we arrived at the B&B. The old, two story, family residence had been turned into a bed and breakfast. We rented two rooms with a shared bath down the hall. Bill and Greg took one room, and the girls and I took the other one.

The rooms were clean and fresh, with simple furnishings, and wood floors. The windows had frilly lace curtains which is part of the culture of the United Kingdom and Europe. The bathroom and toilet (in separate little rooms) were at the end of the hall. Naturally, the kids set out to explore everything. Wyvonna and Shaleen went down the hall to the toilet.

I heard, "Mom, Mom. Come here."

I followed the sound of the voices, and found them in the toilet.

"What do you want?"

"We need some money."

"What do you need money for? You're in the toilet!"

They opened the door. "Come and look at this."

I walked in, and they pointed to a little sign above an open slot on the tank. I am not joking – we had to deposit money to use the toilet! It wasn't much – maybe the equivalent of a dime, but…I couldn't believe it! I started to believe all of the jokes I had heard about how frugal the Scots are. You have to pay to use most public toilets in the UK and Europe, but I still think it's a bit odd that we had to pay in a guest house.

I am reminded of a time Bill and I were in Switzerland. It was in the afternoon, and we had been sightseeing in the vicinity of our hotel when he had to use the toilet. We stopped at a restaurant. He went in and used the toilet. When he came out, the owner of the restaurant was furious.

He confronted Bill and said, "This is not a public toilet."

Bill said, "Well, I am sorry. I didn't know I couldn't use the toilet in a public restaurant. As a matter of fact, we were thinking of returning for dinner tonight, but forget that idea. If you are so hostile over a potential customer using your toilet, then I won't be back." Learning the culture is important.

Here We Go Again

We slept well at the B&B in Scotland. In the morning, we went downstairs for breakfast. The family living room and dining room had been turned into a breakfast area for the guests. There were about five small tables with chairs. The tables had white linen table cloths on them, and were set with pretty dishes. We had a good breakfast of rashers (bacon), eggs, toast, juice, and coffee. I was impressed with the metal rack which held several slices of toast.

After breakfast, we were ready to see as much as possible in the short time we were in Edinburgh. First, we went to the castle. The castle was a favorite place for the royal family to visit. It was large and elegant. The guards wore brightly colored kilts. We saw some men playing bagpipes in their cute little red kilts and hats. I love to hear the bagpipes which are such a well-known part of Scotland.

From the castle, we walked along the "Royal Mile" – Edinburgh's Old Town's busiest tourist street. It is actually a mile of intersecting streets, businesses, and shops. It was originally laid out as a parade ground for the troops - which started at the Castle.

We were walking down the street gawking at everything like normal tourists. The kids and I walked ten steps behind Bill. We prayed no one would think he belonged to us. He was embarrassing us by wearing his souvenir - a silly looking hat with the bright plaid tartan (design) of his family name.

There were many souvenir shops, so we decided to go into another one for the kids to choose something. I saw some tee shirts, and suggested they get one of them. You know how teenagers love different tee shirts. I thought it would be a nice, usable souvenir. The shirt had a picture of a Scotsman, dressed in his colorful Scottish kilt, shirt, and hat. He was holding a fork in one hand and a knife in the other. The caption was, "Haggis Hunter."

A Scotsman saw me looking at the shirt and asked, "Have you ever seen a haggis?"

"No," I answered.

"Are you from America?" he asked.

"Yes." And then he proceeded to educate me. He was so sincere as he described the haggis. He was so friendly, and I appreciated his willingness to explain the local culture and activities to me. I listened with great interest – and I loved hearing the accent.

"A haggis is a little, grey furry animal that lives in the forest in the Highlands. They are about four to fourteen inches in size. They have a long, flat nose something like a duck's bill. Their legs are shorter on one side to enable them to run easily in the mountainous terrain. The law has open season one time a year when hunters can go into the forest and kill them. The "Haggis Hunt" is a popular sport and many like to participate. The haggis' hide in the bush, and are hard to find. Anyone who can bring one home is highly praised, because it takes a lot of skill."

He continued his long story about the haggis, and others who passed by overheard the conversation. Then they would join my "tour guide," and tell even more about the haggis. I was impressed at how friendly they were and how willing to share information with me. I appreciated them, because people are not so helpful and friendly in a lot of countries where we have visited. I could not convince the kids to get the tee shirts, so we left and went on down the street.

We visited an old cemetery, Greyfriars Kirkyard, in the Old Town of Edinburgh. There we saw a statue of a little Skye terrier dog named Bobby. The story was that Bobby belonged to a man named John Gray, who worked for the Edinburgh City Police as a night watchman, and the two were inseparable for approximately two years. John Gray died of tuberculosis on February 8, 1858. He was buried in Greyfriars Kirkyard. Bobby spent the next fourteen years guarding the grave of his owner until Bobby died on January 14, 1872. A wealthy lady had the statue and a fountain erected in memory of Bobby.

We toured the home of the famous reformer, John Knox. There are no written records of the exact year when he was born, but it is thought he was born in 1505. It evoked a special nostalgic feeling in me to be in the study where he created his sermons. He suffered much for his powerful stand on the Bible. His life makes our present Christian lives look so simple and easy. I suggest you would enjoy reading the life of this preacher who sacrificed so much to preach the gospel. John Knox died on November 24, 1572, and was buried in the church yard of the St. Giles' Cathedral where he preached. We were saddened by the disrespect which is apparent at his grave site which is now covered by a paved parking lot. His grave is marked by a small badge between the parking lines of parking space, number 23. He has no monument on earth, but a great reward in Heaven.

We enjoyed our short visit in Edinburgh, and headed back to Coventry. As we were having dinner with our friends that night, we were telling them all about the trip to Scotland. I was still fascinated by the story of the haggis, so I proceeded to tell it to the missionaries. I didn't get far into my story, and they began laughing hysterically.

"Did they ever tell you the truth about the haggis?"

"What do you mean…the truth?"

They enjoyed telling me the haggis is *not* an animal. When the Scots kill an animal for food, they don't waste anything. They cut the meat into all useable pieces. Then they chop all the waste parts of the sheep or pig into small pieces, mix them with a lot of seasoning, clean the stomach of the animal and stuff it with these leftover pieces. It is then sewed up into a round ball. People buy it and slowly boil it. It is traditional and supposed to be delicious. I will take their word for it.

The kids were listening to the true explanation of the haggis, and then verbally pounced on me saying, "Yeah, and you tried to get us to buy those tee shirts. We would have been the laughing stock of Edinburgh to let the Scots see us walking down the street wearing a shirt which says, 'Haggis Hunter'."

The joke was on me, and I could imagine those Scotsmen were still laughing about the naïve American who believed the haggis story.

Since that time, I have enjoyed the experience of seeing a haggis prepared. We were once invited to the home of some Gypsy friends in Hungary for a pig killing. All of the family would get together a couple of times in the year and kill a hog. They would then share the work of cutting and preparing the meat and then divide it between them. I wasn't excited about getting there at four o'clock in the morning to see the pig killed, so we waited until a little later.

They were well organized in the garage, and people worked on different parts of the pig. Some were mixing ground meat for sausage, some were cleaning the intestines in a big bucket of water, and others were cutting chops, bacon, and hams. They taught me how to stuff the sausage meat into the empty intestines. After everything else was done, they took all of the waste parts of the pig and made a haggis.

Our friends took us to Stratford-upon-Avon and to the home of William Shakespeare. I was again thrilled to be *seeing* history. We went to Warwick Castle and toured it. We saw the torture rooms and the supposedly haunted tower. We were enjoying looking at everything in this castle, and we forgot all about time. We realized it was getting late, and we had to leave. We walked outside, and didn't see any other people. The courtyard was empty. We went to the big gate and tried to open it, but it was locked! We spread out, and looked around the castle grounds for a caretaker or another human being who held the keys to the lock. We couldn't find anyone! We had to get out! *What were we going to do?*

We had two choices - sleep on those hard courtyard stones near a haunted tower, and maybe be arrested or climb over the wall! We headed for the high stone wall. Bill, John, and the kids climbed over it without a lot of effort, but I had a problem. I could never even climb a tree, and here I was wearing a skirt and trying to climb over a castle wall! Then I got tickled. Laughing took even more of my energy. Bill finally boosted me from beneath, and John pulled me from the top. They managed to get me over the wall without any injuries. Of course, the kids were laughing and enjoying the episode as much as seeing the castle. I just prayed no one inside - except the ghost - was watching us.

We enjoyed seeing many places of historical interest in England. One of those places was the Blenheim Palace – birthplace of Sir Winston Churchill. He was born in 1874, two months prematurely due to his mother taking a fall while she was visiting in the palace.

Paris

All too soon it was time to leave England and our friends. We flew from London to Paris where we stayed with some missionaries who lived in a suburb of the city. Their schedule was busy at the time, so they showed us how to get on the Metro (subway) and go into Paris to see some of the tourist sites. We didn't have a problem following the directions, and we got into the city early for a full day of adventure.

We first went to the Eiffel Tower – of course! It was hard to believe we were actually looking at the Eiffel Tower! We had to bend our heads back to our shoulders, and look straight up to see the top. The height is equivalent to 81 stories. It is the tallest structure in Paris, and it sets in the middle of a park.

There are three levels for visitors. We paid the fee, went into the tower, and took an elevator to the top. You can walk – if you can! There are three hundred steps between the first and second level and three hundred steps between the second and third level. I didn't plan to die in Paris – so I opted for the elevator. It was almost scary as we stood at the top and looked out over Paris. People and cars at the bottom looked like dots. They had an iron screen around the look-out area to keep people from falling – or jumping.

I was so thankful God was permitting us to see all of those things. We could only have the opportunity to see them as missionaries.

We saw the Triumphal Arch which was commissioned by Napoleon in 1806 to commemorate his victories. He was ousted from power before the arch was completed. It was then built in 1836 during the reign of Louis-Philippe.

We walked down the famous streets of Paris and saw a lot of things – but I didn't see any well-dressed women leading poodles with rhinestone collars! This is supposed to be the fashion capital of the world, but I saw nothing that impressed me.

The day was over, and it was time to return to the home where we were staying. That should be simple – we had directions. However, we found it wasn't as simple as we had thought.

We had problems getting on the trains. We thought we had it figured out, so we went out on the platform and waited for the train. How hard could it be? The trains stopped only for a few seconds while passengers quickly got in and out. We waited until the passengers came out of the train we needed, and then started to enter - but the doors closed. As we pounded and fumbled at the door, the train sped away.

We waited for the next one. This time we had planned our strategy. As soon as the passengers rushed out, we rushed to the door - but it closed again! We quickly looked for a button to

Here We Go Again

push or somehow to open the door. It looked like the doors had opened automatically - but they didn't. We were determined to get into a train. We had to figure it out. We tried about three times, and each time the doors closed before we could board the train. People were sitting on the train watching us and actually laughing at us. Well, I suppose we did look silly, and I probably would have laughed if I had been in their place. We felt like country bumpkins in the city!

But, we were not quitters. Bill took command. He put each of us in a different place. Then he instructed us, "Now if some of you get into the train and the others don't, then just keep trying until you get in one. Then get off at the next stop, and we will meet there. But we are going to figure out how to get into these trains."

We all took our places and waited. The next train stopped, and we watched closely to try to figure out those doors. Then we saw it! When people approached the doors, they slapped a little button on the door - and it opened. So that was the secret! We all managed to get into the same car on the train. Whew! How ignorant can you be? I know there are probably scratch marks on some subway cars in Paris which bear our DNA.

We were looking for our stop, but we missed it! We ended up at the end of the line and had to get off. There was a little village there and some shops. We were hungry, so we bought a loaf of French bread and bottles of water. We ate bread and drank water while trying to figure out the map. Knowledge of the French language sure would have been helpful, because the French people were not. The French think their language is the language of the gods, and if you don't speak French, you are a worthless peasant who doesn't deserve their help. But, with God's help, we found a kind English speaking lady who defied the French culture. (An angel?) She assisted us in getting into the right train.

Bill spoke at the church that night, and told them about our experiences. The French church members had a good laugh about it. I'm sure the people looking at us from inside the trains – well, outside too – are still laughing.

Oh, the memories we have from experiences in foreign countries! Now we would soon be in Kenya. What kind of memories would be created there?

Chapter 2
Welcome to Kenya

Nairobi, Kenya! Many memories came alive. I was happy that we were back under difference circumstances.

It had been many years since we had been in Kenya. We had gone to Nairobi after being forced to leave Asmara, Ethiopia due to the war there. We had served God in Ethiopia, under difficult conditions, until one day Bill came home and announced to me the government had stamped an exit visa in our passports and had given us three days to leave the country. We lived in Eritrea, in the Northern part of Ethiopia. Before World War II, Eritrea had been independent, but had been incorporated into Ethiopia. While we were there, Eritrea was fighting Ethiopia for independence. Also, the Communists were steadily gaining influence in Ethiopia. The country was on the brink of war. In the end, all missionaries were expelled from the country, and the Communists took over the government.

Have you ever tried to pack, sell out, and move in three days? We had to start selling our household furniture, car, and other possessions, pack the personal things, buy tickets, close out all of our business affairs, and be out of Ethiopia in three days - or go to jail. And - where would we go? Back to America? No. Bill had been impressed by the Lord to go to Australia, but we didn't know one person in Australia. We also didn't have visas, and there was no Australian Embassy in Ethiopia. We had to have a visa before leaving. What were we going to do?

We sold and gave away all of our furniture and a lot of our personal things. The rest we packed in 55 gallon barrels, and left them with friends from the U.S. military base. They promised to ship them to us as soon as we got settled in Australia and could provide an address. We also left our vehicle with them to sell.

My emotions, fears, and activity ran full speed during those three days. We had so many things to do to prepare to leave. My nerves were on edge. I was leaving one foreign country and going to another where I didn't know one person. But then my faith took charge. I knew if God wanted us in Australia; He would make the crooked ways straight.

He calmed my troubled soul, and He gave us peace and wisdom in the midst of chaos. (We have learned to thrive on chaos.) We managed to accomplish what we had to do in those three days and flew out of Ethiopia to neighboring Kenya.

We knew we could go to the Australian Embassy in Nairobi and apply for a visa, but we didn't know we had to have someone to sponsor us into the country in order to get a visa. Besides our ignorance of their laws, I have already mentioned that we didn't know anyone in Australia.

One of my life scriptures is (Proverbs 3:5-6), "Trust in the Lord with all thine heart and lean not unto thine own understanding. In all thy ways acknowledge him and he shall direct thy paths." He kept his promise when we arrived in Nairobi.

We got off the plane with our three little children and had no idea where to go. We wandered around the airport - thinking about how to get into the city, and where to go after we got there.

Soon we were approached by a nice American couple. They must have seen the bewilderment in our faces. They introduced themselves, told us he was with the American Embassy, and asked if we needed transportation into town. We thankfully accepted their kind offer. They took us into Nairobi and helped us to find a place to stay. We couldn't afford most of the hotels with our limited budget. They took us to a little, inexpensive hotel which was located on the second floor over a disco. We were grateful to have a place to sleep, and we thanked the couple, and we never saw them again. The music was so loud from the disco we didn't sleep much that night. We knew we had to find another place to stay.

We had heard from missionaries back in Ethiopia that the Mennonite Guest House was a nice place to vacation. We told a taxi driver where we wanted to go, and soon we arrived at the sprawling grounds of the guest house. It was old, and it had been used as quarters for the British military officers during the war. But the American Mennonites had purchased it and had it reconditioned. It was charming and welcoming.

We were able to get a large family room with a private bath for a reasonable price. We paid for room and board which included three meals a day. The meals were served family style in a large, pleasant dining room. The atmosphere was relaxing and peaceful. The children played on the spacious grounds which had beautiful green grass – quite different than our yard in Ethiopia. The staff served us afternoon tea in the lovely garden. This place helped to restore some calmness to us.

The next day we went to the Australian High Commission, and applied for a visa. Again, no one told us about the requirements.

Our stay in Nairobi was much longer than we had anticipated. We sometimes became quite impatient, but we never doubted the visas would be granted. We waited nine long weeks before we received a call from the Australian High Commission. Our visas had been approved! What a miracle! We still didn't know what a miracle we were experiencing until we actually arrived in Australia and learned we should not even be there without a sponsor. We possessed a migrant visa in our passports which allowed us to be in Australia indefinitely! Some people would have paid a lot of money to have that visa - but God! He had promised to never leave us or forsake us – not even in Kenya.

Now, after many years, we were back in Nairobi. We were obeying God's leadership to return to do mission work. Many things had changed. Years ago, Kenya was closed to our mission board, but during the past years it had opened, and now we had several missionaries who were living and working in Kenya.

I was excited when we arrived. This was a new adventure. *Would it be good? What good and bad experiences would our family have in this new country?* I prayed they would be pleasant and profitable for God's work.

Many of the missionaries were at the airport to meet us. We knew most of them. Some of them had been in Ethiopia, and others had been students with us in Bible College. After we loaded all of the bags into the vehicles, we headed towards the Stampers' home in Thika - a few miles on the outskirts of Nairobi. All of the missionaries gathered there for our arrival reception. We were already feeling at home. We knew we were where God wanted us for the time.

While we were enjoying good food and fellowship, we heard a scream from one of the back bedrooms. We all ran towards little Debbie's room. She was crying and almost paralyzed with fear. She had looked up at the ceiling and saw a snake. The men immediately set about to find it and kill it. They did find and kill a Black Mamba – one of the most deadly snakes in Kenya. Welcome to Kenya! TIK. Before dark, the other missionaries left for their homes, and we stayed on with the Stampers.

The next day, Wyvonna, Shaleen, and Greg went with Jon Konnerup and Jay Piercey (other teenaged missionary kids) to explore Nairobi. I was pleased they could quickly make friends and have some activities, so they would not feel so lonely in this new country. Jon and Jay would also be in boarding school with them.

I can recall one custom which stunned them a bit during their orientation that day. They were riding a bus when an African mother nonchalantly started to breast feed her baby – without any kind of cover-up. It was just the beginning of many African experiences which they will remember forever.

We stayed with the Stampers for only a few days. During this time we got our work permits, opened a bank account, and reacquainted ourselves with the city. It had been several years since we had been there, but the city still looked much the same.

The missionaries introduced us to some of the restaurants. We enjoyed a good time of fellowship when they took us to The Steak House, which was located on the second floor of a building in downtown Nairobi. They served great, inexpensive steak with a delicious condiment of white garlic sauce. The Steak House would become one of our favorite places to eat.

We tried to temporarily forget what awaited us in the next few days.

Chapter 3
Tears and Angels

After a few days, the dreaded day arrived when we would take the children to the Rift Valley Academy - the boarding school where they would live until they graduated from high school. Both of our daughters were entering their junior year, and Greg was going into his sophomore year. This was going to be a completely new experience for them, because they had never been away from home for schooling. They had agreed to go to the boarding school before we left the States, but it was only natural for them to have some anxieties. They tried to not show any negative feelings.

I was dreading the day we would have to be separated from the dearest ones to my heart. It was the one thing which had made me hesitate about going to Kenya. I always thought I could never put my kids in boarding school, but there were no other schools where they could attend. They had been home schooled while we traveled, and a couple of the missionaries were home schooling their children on the field. We gave our kids a choice, and they choose RVA. They needed the interaction with other kids their age – even though they were not happy about being separated from us.

RVA was located up in the mountains, near the small town of Kijabe - about one hour from Nairobi - on a plateau overlooking the Great Rift Valley. From the boarding school you could look out over the valley to Longonot, a huge active volcano. The school was old. It had been built by the Sudan Interior Mission to house and to teach the children of missionaries from all over Africa. President Theodore Roosevelt visited Kijabe shortly after leaving office. During his visit in 1909, he laid the cornerstone for Kiambogo – "place of the buffalo." Kiambogo - the main school building - remains the centerpiece of RVA's campus.

RVA was a boarding school for children from grade one through grade twelve. It was the first foreign boarding school in Africa to gain American accreditation.

RVA has quite an interesting history. In 1952, during the Mau Mau emergency, the Mau Mau (a group of vicious revolutionary killers) were raiding and killing white settlers in Kenya. I have been told by reliable sources that the Mau Mau had targeted the school. They thought if they could take the children captive, the British would then do whatever they asked. Whether this is true or not, I do not know, but I do know the following story is documented, and has been told by many who were at RVA on the night of March 28, 1953.

The Mau Mau had been raiding and burning in the area for several days and RVA was the next target. A British officer named "Chipps" was stationed on the campus after high barbed wire had been installed around the compound.

Saturday, March 28, 1953 is one of RVA's greatest stories. Late one afternoon, the staff was tipped off about the plan of the Mau Mau to attack the school. They tried to keep all fearful news from the students, but some of the older students accidently heard the adults discussing the situation. They had no way of getting the information to the authorities to ask for assistance. There were no telephones, and it was too late to try to send someone for help. The students and staff went to bed expecting to be awakened by gunfire in the night. The staff prayed for God's protection, and the attack never happened.

Months later several Mau Mau were captured, and they confessed in court they had been on their way to attack the mission school. When they made their way up the mountain and came within view of the school, they were frightened away, because they saw a large number of soldiers surrounding the complete compound. Historical records show the only British soldier anywhere near Kijabe that night was Chipps. God had sent his angels to protect the school.

This story always gives me goose bumps! It shows how angels manifest themselves as humans. It also gives me comfort to know, "The angel of the Lord campeth round about them that fear him, and delivereth them that fear him," (Psalm 34:7).

There are angels sent from heaven to protect us. (II Kings 6) tells the story about the king of Syria's plan to capture the prophet Elisha. He sent horses, chariots, and a great number of men. They went by night, and compassed the city where Elisha was staying. Elisha's servant arose early in the morning, and saw the city was surrounded. He was afraid, and asked Elisha what they would do. In verses 16-17, Elisha answered, "Fear not: for they that be with us are more than they that be with them. And Elisha prayed, and said, Lord, I pray thee, open his eyes that he may see. And the Lord opened the eyes of the young man; and he saw; and, behold, the mountain was full of horses and chariots of fire round about Elisha." Angels! We would be stunned if God would open our eyes, and let us see our guardian angels. So, why do we fear?

Jon Konnerup and Jay Piercey were returning to RVA, so I was comforted a little – knowing that our kids would know someone there. They had already been having fun with Jon and Jay, so they could go to school together as friends.

The day came when we loaded the kids' suitcases onto the top of Richard Konnerup's Land Rover, and we all piled into the vehicle to make the trek up the mountains to the school. The Land Rover was overloaded with four teenagers, Richard, Bill,

Tears and Angels

and me. Richard's wife, Jeannine, had stayed behind, because there was no room. She knew she would see Jon before long.

We started out through Nairobi, then on to the low road which would take us up into the mountains to Kijabe. Richard went around a curve, and we all gasped as the Land Rover went up on two wheels and almost tipped over. It was definitely overloaded!

We drove for about an hour through small villages, hair pin curves, and then high into the mountains, along the escarpment - a steep cliff which overlooked the Great Rift Valley. There were no guard rails, and one careless maneuver of the driver would have sent us over the cliff and into the valley – straight into Heaven.

We finally came to a small, dirt road where Richard made a right turn which would take us back to RVA. My emotions were building, but I was trying to control my temptation to tell him to turn around and go back to Nairobi. I was getting closer to the reality of leaving my kids on the top of this mountain in the middle of Africa, - and I did not like it.

It was hot, and we had the windows rolled down. The road was dry and dusty. I was getting a headache from breathing the dust which permeated the vehicle. I wished for a mask for my nose and mouth. I prayed, *"Oh, God, please help me to endure this. How can I leave my kids in such a desolate place?"* God reminded me that His grace was sufficient for any situation. I knew God had called us to Kenya, and He had dealt with me specifically about this moment.

My silent tears were mixing with the dust as we finally came to a little crude underpass. When we went through the underpass, we entered the RVA compound. Near the underpass, we passed one of the boys' dorms. It was a very old, long building with a low roof. I silently prayed, "Lord, please don't let Greg be assigned to that dorm." We then followed the road around to Kiambogo in the center of the compound. Jon was pointing out different buildings, and giving an orientation of the compound. There was a lot of activity as parents unloaded their kids' suitcases, and the usual excitement as friends greeted each other after being apart for the year-end break.

We went to the office to check in and to get the kids' dorm assignments and all the other information. To my disappointment, Greg was assigned to the old dorm building which we had driven past – new kid on the plateau. I felt deflated. I was so hoping he would be assigned to one of the newer dorms, but it was not to be. Wyvonna and Shaleen would be rooming together in a newer two-story dorm.

We took care of all the paper work, and then went around to the dorm to unload Greg's things. We parked at the end of the building, and I gathered up some of his things. I made my way down the narrow, dingy hallway to his room. My heart sank as I walked into the room. It was so small! It was the smallest room in the dorm. There was a single bed on either side with about four feet between them. A chest of drawers for each boy sat under the window between the beds. A small closet was on each side at the foot of the beds. That was it! It looked more like a jail cell. Greg's roommate, a Norwegian boy named Carston, was sitting on his bed. He was leaning up against the wall with his stereo next to him. He looked like he had been abandoned by the world.

I was in tears as I went back to the Land Rover where Bill and Greg were getting the rest of his luggage.

I took Bill aside and said, "Bill, I can't leave him here in this horrible place. That room is like a jail cell. There is no space in it. I just can't leave him here."

Bill replied in a truly male way, "What do you want to do – make a sissy out of him? I didn't have that much when I went in the Army. He'll be fine. Now, don't let him see you are upset."

I was amazed later at the resilience of teenagers with a good attitude. When Greg came home for a visit, I questioned him about the room. To my surprise, he said, "Oh, my room is the most popular room in the dorm. We have fixed it up so nice, and all the boys want it." So much for the emotions of a mother!

We then went to the girls' dorm where we found Wyvonna and Shaleen's room on the second floor. It was simple, but it was much more spacious than Greg's room. We did a bit of interchanging from other rooms to get good chest of drawers for them. We had brought sheets and a bed cover from the States for all three of the kids, so we made the beds and arranged the room. It looked pretty nice - for a dorm room in the wilderness of Africa!

Some of the kids took us on a tour around the campus. Most of the buildings were quite old, with the exception of two or three newer dorms. They explained a lot about the school and the activities. Each dorm had a small apartment for a dorm parent, which was usually a married couple. Wyvonna and Shaleen had a single, female missionary as their dorm parent.

Finally, the time came when we had to say goodbye and leave the kids there. It almost ripped my heart out. All of the students seemed friendly, and I knew it wouldn't be hard for our kids to make friends quickly. There were a few parting tears, but the kids were brave, and tried not to show a lot of emotion. (Shaleen cried *after* we left.)

In the beginning of our missionary ministry, I was pious – I thought it was commendable.

Some people would say, "Oh, you have to make so many sacrifices to be a missionary."

I would answer (in all my piety), "Oh, we don't sacrifice anything compared to what Jesus sacrificed for us."

Well, that is true – but for me, leaving our children in boarding school on the top of an African mountain, was a huge sacrifice! Only the love of Christ could constrain me to do it! I don't think I could have had the faith and obedience of Abraham. God told me to LEAVE my children on a mountain – but God told Abraham to KILL his son on a mountain. God said without faith it is impossible to please Him (Hebrews 11:6), and I was trying to have the faith that God would take care of my children. Easy? NOOOOO!!

I prayed for strength, grace, and peace. I had to try to settle down and set my mind for the challenge ahead of me.

Chapter 4
Frustration, Fun, and Friends

Soon after taking the kids to RVA, we went back up the mountain to Brackenhurst, the Southern Baptist language school just outside of Limuru, which was about fifty miles North of Nairobi, and about thirty minutes from RVA.

Brackenhurst was previously a one hundred year old farm which had been a grant in 1912 from King George the Fifth of England to a Mr. Charles Major. Mr. Major sold it in 1914 to the Hudson Cane family who had emigrated from England. The Canes built the main house and several cottages on the property. They named it "Three Tree Farm" because of the trees which were standing at that time. The name was later changed to Brackenhurst – which speaks of past and present. During World War II, Brackenhurst was used for a lodge. The Southern Baptists purchased it in 1964 and turned it into a world conference center. When we arrived in 1980, the compound was used primarily for a language school and a conference center for the Southern Baptists.

Richard Konnerup took us to the school, and introduced us to those in charge. Richard and all of our other missionaries had studied at Brackenhurst when they arrived in Kenya. We and Richard and Jeannine had studied at another mutual language school – in Addis Ababa, Ethiopia. We had know the Konnerups since Bible College days, and then served with them in Ethiopia.

We had previously done all the paperwork for enrollment at Brackenhurst, so the people at the school were expecting us.

After the introductions and a bit of orientation, we were taken to the cottage where we would be living for the next six months. Our cottage was near the main building which housed the dining hall. Our temporary home was old – one of the original buildings. It was a bigger shock than the kids' accommodations at RVA. The outside was a small, white washed, plastered structure with a low roof. Inside, there was a small sitting room, crude kitchen, and two small bedrooms. One bedroom had a single bed and a bunk bed. This was the room our kids would share when they visited us. Home! The walls were white, and the floors were rough wood. The furniture was adequate, but plain and sparse. My heart sank a little, but I knew I had no choices, and that God would give me enduring grace for the next six months.

God Sent a Friend to Me

Richard drove away, and we started to unpack our suitcases. I was determined to make this place as pleasant as possible. I walked outside, and saw a pretty, smiling young woman making her way towards me. She came up and introduced herself as Cheryl Camp. She was so warm, friendly, and bubbly. I immediately felt a kindred spirit with her. She and her husband, Carroll, were missionaries with the Southern Baptists, and they had transferred to Kenya from Uganda. They had two young children; Matthew was six years old, and Lauren was four. The friendship which began that day has lasted over these past thirty one years.

Cheryl was from Augusta, South Carolina, and she had a sweet southern accent and personality plus. She had been at Brackenhurst for about two months waiting for language school. She had become familiar with the area and offered to help me with shopping, getting the cottage livable, or anything she could do. She invited us to have dinner with them that night. They lived in a newer duplex at the top of the hill. It was a simple, concrete block structure, but it looked like a palace compared to our cottage. We had such a good time of fellowship with them. I know God sent her to me when I really needed a friend.

A short time later, the Southern Baptist missionaries, who occupied the other side of their duplex, moved on to their mission station. These units were usually reserved for SB missionaries, but Cheryl and Carroll went to bat for us. They talked to the right people, and soon we moved from our primitive cottage to the duplex (mansion) on the hill – next door to the Camps. We were so grateful. We still had only two bedrooms, but the unit was much newer and more modern than the previous cottage. We felt it would be a much better place for our children when they were able to visit with us.

Our friendship with the Camps made our time at Brachenhurst bearable. We just seemed to click immediately, and became good friends. Being able to laugh together eased a lot of the stress of language study. We became, and still are, Uncle Bill and Aunt LaMoin to Matthew and Lauren.

I dressed much plainer in Kenya than I do in the States, but I still liked to look nice. I don't remember what I had done one day which prompted little Lauren to say to her Mom, with her sweet southern drawl, "Aunt LaMoin just likes to be fannncy." That has been a family joke since then. They have been back in the States for several years now, and we try to see each other as often as our schedules allow. Lauren is now married and has her own daughter and lives in South Carolina. When her daughter was born, I sent her a lovely, frilly dress. I told Lauren, "You have to make this child *fancy*." Matthew is now a brilliant reconstructive plastic surgeon working for Mayo Clinic.

A Screw in the Cornbread

I did our cooking in our own living quarters, but Brackenhurst had a large dining room where we could pay a small amount for meals. One night we decided to have dinner there with some friends. I can't remember anything which we had for dinner that night except big pieces of beautiful cornbread. Since I am a southerner, I love cornbread.

We were all eating, talking, and having a wonderful time. I took a bite of cornbread, and when I started to chew it, a pain shot through my teeth, and tears came to my eyes. *Ouch.* I had bitten down on something hard and painful. I forgot about manners and spit the mouthful of cornbread into my hand – and saw a huge metal screw! TIK. My teeth and jaw were sore for about three days, and later half of my back molar broke away. No, you don't sue for such a thing in Africa. For the past twenty-five years, every time I go to a dentist, he/she asks, "Did you know half of your back molar is gone?" The tooth has never bothered me, so I haven't spent the money on a crown. *That is one of my marks of a missionary!*

Swahili Was a Challenge

It had been a long time since we had been in language school, and we had mixed emotions. We were looking forward to it, but Bill was feeling some dread, because he has always labored to learn foreign languages. He had to work much harder, because he has no natural gift for language as some do.

School started, and we were in the classroom with about six other couples. One couple had been missionaries in Kenya for several years. They had never had formal instruction in the language, but they could speak a lot of it already. Some of the other couples were fresh out of college. They were smart and still in the learning mode. The Camps had pastored for some years

Frustration, Fun, and Friends

before going to Uganda, but they were younger and bright. Bill was in his 50's – never mind how old I was! So, we had our work cut out for us.

I was progressing and trying to enjoy the instruction, but one thing I detested was the lab work. They would sit us in a cubical with head phones, and we had to listen to tapes of Swahili for about two hours. I knew the reason was to get us used to hearing the sounds of the language, but it was so boring when I couldn't understand anything. I resented this part of the study, but I knew I had to do it, so I tried to make the best of it.

We were instructed to go into Nairobi on week-ends so we could practice our Swahili. I enjoyed this assignment, because it took us into the city for awhile. Beautiful escape! However, we quickly encountered a problem with using Swahili. We would go to a restaurant, speak Swahili to the servers, and they would respond in English! They wanted to use their English as much as we wanted to use Swahili. Of course, you must realize that the British occupied Kenya for many years, and English was the common language during that time. In fact, English is still the government language. It was spoken by most Kenyans in Nairobi.

We had a Kenyan instructor who was a bit prideful and arrogant. Mutsoli liked to teach by intimidation. I also think he secretly didn't like any of us. It took a lot of patience and grace to keep from trying to choke him. In spite of all the obstacles, we were progressing well and keeping up with the young scholars. Then, after about a month, Bill came down with Malaria! He had contracted it in Ethiopia years before, but it never leaves the body. He had a bad flare-up of it. He was too sick to go to school or to study at home. He was sick for two weeks - which was disastrous. You cannot miss even one day in language school. The lessons have so much material that it's almost impossible to catch up with the class if you miss a few days. Bill struggled after he was able to go back to class.

I was doing quite well in the language study, but felt so sorry for Bill in his struggles that it greatly affected me. I did not want to make him feel badly, so I lost my zeal for trying to excel in the language.

The Camps were suffering from some culture shock, and we tried to be an encouragement to them. They went into Uganda during difficult times in the country, and later transferred to Kenya, because they didn't want to keep their children in Uganda. We took them with our family to Nairobi to spend Thanksgiving Day with Larry and Michele Stringfield, who were missionaries with our mission.

Michele was an awesome cook, and they were fun people. They had four children and two Poodle dogs. There was always excitement and chaos there. We ate, laughed, and had a wonderful time. Our children enjoyed being away from RVA for a couple of days, and they always laughed at the antics of Larry and Michele. When they got bored, they would say, "Let's go out to the Stringfields and watch the show."

Everytime something frustrating or unusual happened, Larry would say, "TIK" or "That's TIKish." We asked what it meant, and he said, "This Is Kenya." In the future, we used the phrase when something upset us, or made us laugh. It just seemed to fit so many situations and helped to remove a little of the stress.

Michelle and Larry lived in a coffee plantation on the outskirts of Nairobi. They had guard dogs and a night watchman. They purchased a good guard dog, and soon afterwards a leopard came on the compound one night and killed the dog and their milk cow. They were always in the middle of some stressful situation. It was entertaining just to listen to them tell about what had happened since we last saw them.

Many of us gathered at their house for a holiday. The women were sitting at the table talking when their little boy, Micah, came to the table. He was about four years old.

He went to Michelle, and he said calmly, "Mama, I have a pin up my nose."

"A pin up your nose? How did you get a pin up your nose?"

"I stuck it up there."

Michelle panicked, "Oh, my goodness, oh, my goodness. Was the pin open?"

"Yes." Michelle was almost beside herself. She grabbed him and started trying to look up his nose. I was watching this scene and thinking, *if he had an open pin up his nose, he wouldn't be so calm.*

I said, "Michelle, he's okay. He's not crying. If he had an open pin up his nose, he would be in pain."

I pulled him over by me and said, "Micah, you didn't put a pin up your nose, did you?"

He then grinned and said, "No. I was just kidding."

I think he just wanted to see what kind of reaction he would get from everyone. I'll never know why he thought of telling us that story, unless Michelle had warned him to never put anything in his nose. There was never a dull moment.

Stuck on the Mountain

Richard Konnerup let us use his little Italian car while we were at Brackenhurst. He had installed a switch underneath the dash which turned the ignition on and off so it could not be stolen. One day we drove up the mountain to visit the kids. We were returning home late in the afternoon, and the engine stopped running. Bill pulled over on the side of the road, lifted the hood, but couldn't see anything wrong. He adjusted a couple of things, came back, and tried to start the car. It wouldn't start. He worked for about a half hour trying to find out what was wrong with it. It was getting dark, and we were concerned. It wasn't safe to be on the roads at night. Of course, we didn't have cell phones back then to call for help. He was looking under the hood again, and I was praying.

Suddenly, the Lord said to me, "*Check the switch.*"

The switch, Lord? It wasn't turned off.

"*Check the switch.*" I checked the switch, and it *was* turned off! My knee must have bumped it, but I was not aware of it. *Oh, no. Bill is going to kill me.*

He came back to the window - disgusted and frustrated.

I said, "Try it one more time, and maybe it will start."

"I've tried it over and over. It's not going to start. I don't know what's wrong with it. We sure don't need to be struck on this mountain at night."

"I've been praying it would start, so please, just try it."

Reluctantly, and in a state of frustration, he got in the car and turned the key. Zoommmmm – it started. TIK.

Oh, thank you Lord. I silently said with a sigh of relief.

Bill looked at me and said, "You turned that switch off, didn't you?"

"Now, WHY would I do that?"

"Well, you must have accidently hit it with your knee, but you turned it off."

I never did admit knowing I must have turned it off. I told him after a couple of weeks!

Our First Christmas in Kenya

We persevered in the language study until our Christmas break. The kids were also breaking for Christmas, and they were coming "home" for the month long holiday. We started to try to do some Christmas shopping. There wasn't much to buy for their gifts, and we were also working on a limited budget. It wasn't cheap to pay for language school and for the kids' schooling at RVA.

We went to the big market in Nairobi. There is one large building which houses individual native shops. The large market is surrounded by many smaller, open-air markets. The big building has two floors, and there are thousands of wood carvings, baskets, native jewelry, and many other things which catch the interest of the naïve tourist.

We always had to do some hard bargaining on the prices. My Dad was an expert in this field, and he taught me well. Of course, I then earned my advanced degree in Ethiopia. I loved the challenge of it. If they asked me 100 shillings, I would offer 20.

"Oh, Madame, that is less than I paid for it. Okay, I give you a good price. Give me 80 shillings."

I would put my hand over my heart and say, "You are killing me. Please take me to the hospital." They would laugh.

Then I would say, "Okay, I'll give you 30 shillings."

They would come down a bit, and I would go up a bit. I intended to get the item for about 40 shillings.

When the man or lady would refuse to come down any more, I would say, "Okay. I understand if you can't sell it any cheaper, so I will look around." I would start to walk away. If they didn't call me back, I knew their price was at the bottom, but most of the time as I was walking, I could hear them calling, "Okay, okay, Madame. Come back." They would look sad as I was paying for it – which was all a part of bargaining.

I have seen tourists come in, and pay the first asking price – which to them was cheap. When they walked away, the Africans would have a good laugh. TIK.

Bill usually ended up feeling sorry for the Africans, but I was harder. I knew they were probably still making a great profit or they wouldn't sell it.

We finally bought a big, carved elephant for Greg and "Matatus" for Wyvonna and Shaleen. A Matatu was a vehicle similar to a pickup truck with a top on the back. They were painted with bright decorations. The word "Matatu" meant "three cents a ride." The Kenyans used them for a taxi or bus. There were long bench seats on both sides and a door in the back. They packed people into those vehicles until arms were sticking out the windows, and two or three would be hanging onto the back with legs dangling off the sides. There would be bundles of all sorts on the top, sometimes including some live chickens or animals.

It was so hilarious to watch the vehicle stop for another passenger. It would already be overloaded, sometimes leaning precariously to one side, but they would actually push people into the open back door. Their heads would be inside, their hind parts sticking out the back, and their hands gripping any solid surface to keep from falling. The matatu "conductor" would keep pushing bodies in until there was no possible way to push another one in through the back door. Sometimes three back sides would be sticking out the back. TIK. Because of the weight, it would almost be dragging on the road. The kids laughed about them a lot, so we thought it would be something they could keep and appreciate when they left Kenya.

Greg's bull elephant was a beautiful wood carving, but they had included all of the body parts underneath. We didn't think it looked nice, so after the kids opened their gifts on Christmas Eve, Bill got a hammer and chisel and started to castrate that elephant! He carefully chipped away on it late at night. The next morning, the Camps asked, "What were you doing last night? We kept hearing a weird sound like chipping." TIKish.

The Norfolk Hotel in Nairobi

The Norfolk Hotel was steeped in history. It was the first hotel in Nairobi. It opened on Christmas Day 1904, offering elegance and comfort in the wilds of Africa. White settlers were just coming into Kenya, and this provided a place to stay, socialize, and plan many explorations of the region. The "safari" was born in the Norfolk. President Theodore Roosevelt stayed in the hotel, and began his world famous safari there in 1909. Nairobi grew up around the Norfolk.

On New Years Day, we awoke with the terrible news of a terrorist attack in Nairobi. A bomb was planted in the Norfolk by an Arab guest. It exploded during a New Year's Eve dinner, killing twenty people and injuring eighty. It destroyed one wing of the hotel. The results were chaotic. The need for blood was being broadcast on the radio and by word of mouth. Many tourists were among those who were killed or injured.

Responsibility for the attack was claimed by an Arab group who was seeking retaliation for Kenya's allowing Israeli troops to refuel in Nairobi during the raid on Entebbe Airport in Uganda four years earlier to rescue hostages from a hijacked airplane.

The hotel rebuilt, but lost some of its history. The movie, "Out of Africa" was filmed while we were in Nairobi. The cast stayed in the Norfolk.

The Lord Led Us to the Indians

On the weekends, we went into Nairobi to look for a house. We already knew the Lord was leading us to work with the huge Indian population in the city. We had been burdened for them when we stayed nine weeks there on our way from Ethiopia to Australia.

At that time we were impressed by the thousands of Indians in the city. They had been brought in from India in the early 1900s to help to build the railroad. They found a good life in Kenya and stayed. Others left the over populated country of India, and migrated to Kenya for a better life. They were good business people and hard workers. After the Kenyans gained independence from the British, the Indians quickly gained control of the economy. The women looked a bit out of place in this African city, but so elegant in their beautiful, flowing saris.

We were surprised no missionaries were trying to get the gospel to them. We knew the work would be much harder and slower than working with the Africans. The Indians were all Hindu, Sikh, and Muslim - and religious. They were also connected in family and community, so there was much persecution if one left their religion. But we knew the Lord was leading us to work with them. Someone had to try to get the gospel to them.

Most of the Indians spoke English. Furthermore, most of the people in Nairobi spoke English, so we began to wonder if we really needed to stay at Brackenhurst and labor with the language study. We were a bit frustrated, because the school was expensive, and we felt we were wasting time and money. We prayed about it, and finally decided to move on into Nairobi and begin our ministry with the Indians.

Chapter 5
Our Home in Nairobi

It was not easy to find a house that we could afford. There was a large population of expatriates (foreigners) who lived in the city, and worked for the many foreign embassies and other companies. They rented most of the good houses, and paid high prices for rent. Therefore, the rent standard for houses was usually based on what they paid, and I can assure you they made a lot more money than we did.

We finally found a townhouse near the Westland's Shopping Center. It was the middle unit in a triplex owned by an Indian, and it was located in a quiet area on a road which went back to an extension of the university. I was not happy when I looked at it. There was a small kitchen and an L-shaped dining room and living room downstairs, and three bedrooms and a bath upstairs. The space was okay. There was adequate room for the kids when they were home, but it was difficult for me to visualize anything remotely pretty from what I saw. The walls were painted bright colors – red, green, and blue. The doors were all black. There was a horrible, home made partition between the living room and the dining room. It looked so closed in and depressing.

"No, I cannot live in this place."

"The owner said they would repaint it, and we can remove the partition," Bill argued.

"No way. This is horrible! Paint will never fix it."

"You must visualize the way it can look."

"No visualization can improve this place."

I absolutely refused to consider it, so we continued our search. But, after exhausting our efforts to find anything else which was acceptable and affordable, Bill suggested going back to have a second look at the townhouse. I was beaten down and tired, so I agreed. When we returned, the landlord was not home, so we could not go inside. However, the Indian renter next door offered to show us her unit. It was the same as the one in the middle we had looked at, but hers was much more pleasant. She had it nicely painted and decorated, and I could finally visualize what the other unit could look like with a transformation.

The owner agreed to remove the partition and to repaint the entire house to our specifications. We agreed on a price for the rent, and put down a deposit. We finally had a home, and soon we could feel settled, and start the work which God had called us to do.

I felt liberated when we were able to move our things from Brackenhurst to the newly decorated, beautiful townhouse. The new paint had transformed it, and I was so happy with the results. Our shipment had arrived from the States with all of our personal household things, and we were able to buy a nice table and chairs for the dining room, living room furniture, and things for the bedrooms. After I made curtains, put up pictures, and other decorations, the place really looked nice.

We brought the kids home for a weekend, and they were happy to finally have a home and their own space. It was also convenient for them because they were allowed to come to Nairobi occasionally on a school bus which dropped them off at the Westland's Shopping Center. They could spend the day in Nairobi, and then take the bus back in the afternoon. Sometimes they would bring their friends to our house, and it was easy to get them back to catch the bus. Usually, we would let them stay a little longer, and we would drive them back to RVA. They were also allowed to come home for two weekends during each three month term.

Mary Joined Our Family

Every compound had a place for the servants to live. Now, don't get uptight over the mention of servants. Almost everyone, foreign and middle class Kenyans, employed people to work in their homes. That was part of the culture. It also provided work for the poor Kenyans. We didn't have all of the "servants" which you have in America – washing machines, dish washers, etc. – so we had someone to help us in those areas. This provided more time which we could devote to the ministry and family. We also had servants' quarters on the compound which came with the house.

We soon hired Mary, a rotund, pleasant woman, who would become dear to our family. Mary and her husband and children moved into the quarters at the back. I had red and white checked gingham dresses and white aprons made for Mary to wear. Like all Kenyan women, she added a white scarf to her head, and she looked like Aunt Jemima. Mary was a blessing. She had worked for American missionaries in the past, so she could speak English. She also did a little cooking. Her specialty was cinnamon rolls – she made the best I've ever eaten. Mary had a lot of knowledge of our culture, so she understood us a little better than most of the servants. She knew how we liked things. She also had a good sense of humor.

One day Mary walked past the floor length mirror at the end of the hall. She hesitated, stood, and looked at herself. The Kenyans usually didn't have mirrors in their homes, so she wasn't used to seeing herself. (She didn't know Bill was watching.)

She turned one way and then another way and said, "Mmmm, mmmm, where did dat body come from?" She quickly became loved by our whole family, and she loved us and our children. She taught me much about the Kenyan culture and the people.

Life is seldom boring in Africa. It's the same with life anywhere – you never know what is waiting for you in the next day. But in Kenya, the experiences were sure to be unusual, frustrating, and entertaining. It was good to keep in mind, "This is the day the Lord has made, let us rejoice and be glad in it." Some of my coming experiences required discipline of the mind.

Chapter 6
Plants, Actors, and a Piece of Junk

I was shopping in Westland's one day, when I saw a young man selling rubber plants. I examined them. The roots had damp fresh dirt, and the leaves were healthy and shiny. I had wanted some plants, so I bought them. I took them home and planted and watered them well. We had to go out of town for a few days, and when we returned my plants were dead. All the leaves were on the floor. I was so disappointed.

Mary asked, "Where did you get those plants?"

"At Westland's," I replied. She started to laugh.

"Mama, those are not plants. You should have asked me first."

"What do you mean? They have roots, stems, and leaves."

She took them outside, pulled them out of the pots, and proceeded to remove the dirt from the stems. To my utter astonishment, she showed me some red plastic string tied around the roots. When she removed the string, I could see where the young man had cut the limbs off a rubber tree, spliced them to roots of other weeds, tied them together, and packed dirt around the string. TIK.

I was furious! After I vented for a few minutes, I suddenly stopped and started laughing. Mary looked at me as if I was crazy. But I then realized how creative the guy had been in order to make money. I admired his dishonest ingenuity.

About a month after that incident, I was back at Westland's when the same young man approached me and tried to sell me two more rubber plants. I was surprised he didn't recognize me, because they had unbelievable memories. I pretended to be interested in the plants. I took one from him, looked all over it, and I began to pick the dirt from the stem where I knew it would be spliced together. He reached for it, but I held on to it. When I revealed the string, he became nervous.

"You are a crook. You sold me two of these plants, and you cheated me. I am going to call the police."

"Oh, madam, these are not my plants. They belong to a friend. I sell strawberries." TIK .

I laughed, and felt compensated that I had exposed his trickery, and I let him go – with a stern warning which was useless.

A Wonderful Actor

A lot of things happened at Westland's. Our post office was there, so we were there almost daily. One day after we got the mail, we went outside and were sitting in the car reading it. A man walked up to my side of the car and knocked on the window. I rolled it down, and he started telling me the saddest story. It seemed he had just gotten discharged from the Kenyan army, and he was told that his wife – who was living in their home village – had given birth to a baby. As he told me the story, he started to cry.

"My wife died in childbirth. I don't know if the child lived or not. I need to go there, but I don't have the money. I have some money, but it is not enough for the bus fare. All I need is a few more shillings. Will you please help me?" By this time, tears were streaming down his face.

I looked at Bill, and he said, "I'm not giving him anything. He is lying."

My heart was touched. "But what if he isn't lying?"

"LaMoin, the man is lying. I am not going to give him any money. Now, if you want to give him the money, okay, but I am not giving him a shilling."

"Well, he sounds so sincere, and maybe he is telling the truth. I would hate to not help him if he is telling the truth." Bill just shook his head and smiled.

I gave him the money, and he bowed and thanked me over and over. We drove on home, and I felt good about helping the man. Later in the afternoon some of our missionary friends, Richard and Darlene Clark, came to visit us.

During our conversation, Darlene said, "We were just down at Westland's, and we heard the saddest story. A man came to the car, and told us he had just gotten out of the army, and he had learned his wife had died in childbirth in their village up country. He was crying and trying to get just a few more shillings to get the bus to go there. We felt so sorry for him and gave him the money." TIK.

We Bought a Piece of Junk

We were now settled into our house, and the time came to return the little borrowed car to Richard, so we needed to get our own vehicle. We didn't have much money, and we could not afford to pay for an expensive car. We prayed that the Lord would provide this desperate need.

One day we went out to visit with the Stringfields. Another missionary had left his old Volkswagen van at their house when he left Kenya. We asked Larry about it, and he said Dennis wanted to sell the van. He said it needed some work done on it (an understatement), but we could get it for a cheap price. We had a friend who was a mechanic, and he would help Bill to do the work on it, so we bought it for a few hundred dollars.

The missionary had left a lot of junk in the van, so we proceeded to clean it out – which took a lot of time. It looked bad before we cleaned it out, but it looked worse after we could see it. It was pathetic, but Bill felt he could fix it up. He finally got it started, and we drove it home.

I had to be careful where I put my feet in the floor, because it was all rusted out. The holes were so big I could see the road underneath my feet. I had to keep quoting the scripture to myself about "casting down imaginations." I thought, *if the floor is that bad underneath my feet, what is it like under my seat?* I could almost imagine myself hanging down on the road – seat and all – while we were driving. There was no doubt I would lose a lot of weight if that happened. We managed to get home without my feet, or all of my body, dropping through to the road.

When the kids came home and saw it, they were shocked. "Mom, why did you let him buy that piece of junk? That's almost like letting him get away with murder."

Bill pulled the engine out of it later and rebuilt it. He welded pieces of metal over the rusted out floor. We kept it patched together and drove it for a couple of years.

I remember we took the kids to a game reserve once in that van. It was hysterical! We had to turn off the main road onto a rough dirt road to get back to the cabin where we were to spend the night. We were bouncing along when we heard a sound like something dragging underneath the van. Bill stopped and checked. It was a shock which had come loose and was dragging on the road. He tied it up, and we continued down the road. After a short distance, we heard it again. He got out, and put it back. This happened about four times. He finally found a piece of wire and managed to wire it back in place so we could finish the trip. The girls were laughing hysterically to keep from dying of embarrassment. They said, "Here come the Cunninghams."
TIK

One time when we stopped to repair the shock, the girls had to go to the toilet.

I told them, "Just go over there behind that tree. It will be okay."

After we returned to Nairobi, we read in the paper about a man who was mauled by a lion about the same place where they went to the toilet. Their angels were camped around about them!

The old van was a piece of junk, but it provided a lot of laughs for us. In the beginning, when we were cleaning it, we found an old diary which Dennis had written when he was a missionary in Ethiopia. He told about flying to Addis Ababa from his interior mission station. The Ethiopians operated a small local airline – of sorts. The schedules and the service left a lot to be desired.

Dennis wrote, "I flew to Addis today. I hurried to do my business and shopping. I wanted to get back to the airport early, so I would take no chance on missing the flight back home. I hurried back to the airport and got there an hour early, and that cotton-pickin plane had already left."

Another entry: "I knew this was going to be a bad day when Lois fell out of the attic this morning." We needed some humor.

Chapter 7
They Wrapped Me in Six Yards of Cloth

We met a large number of Indians before we moved to the city, so we proceeded to get closer to them in hopes we could get them to hear the gospel. We attended all social functions which we were invited to. We tried to merge into their culture in any way we could that would not violate our Christian convictions. We went to their weddings, ate in their homes, and even visited a couple of Hindu temples. Winning the Hindus required first forming a friendly relationship with them. When they trusted us as friends, they would listen to what we told them about God.

We looked for a building to rent to start the church, but we couldn't locate one. After some time, we started having church in our home. It was crowded, but we moved the furniture around on Sunday so we could set up folding chairs. Bill made a small removable pulpit that he would carry in on Sunday. Upstairs, at the end of the hallway, there was a door which opened to a balcony. I taught Sunday school there.

We became good friends with Simon, who was an Indian of mixed blood. His wife Carol was half British and half African. He rode a big Honda Gold Wing, and he worked as a mechanic for the Honda Company. They started coming to church with their three children. Through them we met many more Indians, and we learned much about their culture and religions. Soon, we were packing our living room with people on Sunday morning.

We used many methods to get close to the Indians so we could witness to them. We quickly learned to love the Indian food. It was so delicious; I could have eaten it every day. The Indians tried to teach me how to cook it, but I never managed to get the same taste in the food. Some of the Indian women gave me beautiful saris, and they taught me how to wear them. I used to think I could never wrap six yards of cloth around my body and walk in it without it falling off - or without tripping over it. But I learned to wear them. I felt so elegant in a sari. I learned to prefer them to western clothing, and I wore them to all of the Indian functions.

My English Class

I started to teach a class of thirteen women who wanted to improve their English. We met twice a week for English lessons. I used the children's correspondence courses from Source of Light to teach them. While I taught them better English, I was also teaching them the Bible, and they loved the Bible stories. One of the ladies came to me one day and told me her father-in-law was in the hospital. When she visited him, she read the stories to him. So, my teaching was reaching into areas where I could never enter – through my students.

I became acquainted with the families through this class. One day, a well educated, beautiful married daughter of one of the ladies called me.

She said, "My grandmother has died, and we are sitting with her through the time of mourning. Will you come?"

I was surprised and honored that I would be invited into such a private time. Usually no outsiders were invited to participate in this time of mourning. I went to the home and offered my condolences to the entire family. The house was full of family and friends. The ladies all sat together in one room.

After being there for a short time, I started to leave, but they wouldn't let me. They insisted I stay with them. I sat with them and ate with them for most of the day. They knew my heart was with them. I was letting my light shine, and they saw Christ in me.

I believe some of those ladies became believers in our Lord Jesus Christ, but they could never make a public profession. Nor could they ever come to our church. Why? In the Indian culture, when a young man marries, he takes his bride to live in his family home. In Nairobi, the Indians controlled the economy. Most of them owned the stores in town, and everyone worked in the family business. The sons were trained to follow in the steps of their fathers. They took over the business when the father passed on. In the extended family, they all live together and work together – and worship together. If one of those ladies had let it be known that she had converted to Christianity, her husband would have divorced her and cast her out of the family home. She would also have been shunned by the community. She would have no home, no children, and no money. Therefore, fear kept them from publically confessing their belief in Christ. I wonder how easy it would have been for me to receive Christ if I had been an Indian.

Americans do not understand what prices people pay in other countries to become Christians. I enjoyed being with these ladies and teaching them. I learned a lot about them and loved them. I think I will see some of them in Heaven.

When the Indian bride goes to live in her husband's home, her mother-in-law rules over her. To the casual onlooker, their lives look so ideal. The mother, father, sons, and their wives and children all live in one large home. They share the work, help to raise the children, eat and play together. How wonderful! No, it is not wonderful. The wives of some of those men suffer many abuses. They are almost like servants.

I sat next to an Indian woman on a plane once. I started a conversation, and she was friendly. She told me her story.

She lived in Bombay, India. She was the "victim" of an arranged marriage. When she was young, she and a young man were in love. But each of them had to go through with a marriage which was arranged by their parents. She conformed and married - without love. She was miserable in the home of her in-laws. Her father-in-law died. Her mother-in-law made her life miserable. She raised children to adulthood in that home. Finally, her mother-in-law and her husband died on the same day. No, she did not murder them. However, she was happy and relieved. She felt she had been set free – almost.

Her adult son assumed the role of his father. The mother and son ran a printing business together. They were rich. But, the poor woman was not happy. When a husband dies in India, the widow is considered the same as dead. They used to burn them with their husbands, but the law now forbids that barbaric practice. However, they must live a life of almost seclusion. They are never allowed to go to parties, wear jewelry or make-up, or wear any clothing that is not black – for the rest of their lives!

This lady had been in contact with the man she had loved as a young woman. He lived in Chicago, and his wife was gone also. She lied to her son, and told him she was going to visit friends in Canada. Instead, she bought a ticket to Chicago. She told me if she and the man still had those feeling of love for each other, they would marry.

Before the plane landed, she went to the restroom and put on make-up and her jewelry. She looked pretty. After we landed, we went to retrieve our luggage. As we were leaving the conveyer, she brought her friend and introduced him to us. They were holding hands when they walked away. I think they still had feelings for each other. This is one happy story out of many thousands of sad ones.

Our First Muslim Convert

We visited in one home where we met a man who was in a wheelchair. He and his wife were Muslims. After a few visits, we led them to the Lord. He wanted a Bible, so we gave him one. He read it from cover to cover. He wanted to come to church, so Bill would drive to his home and carry him and his wheelchair down a flight of stairs to the van and take him to church. They were poor because of his physical handicap, but his wife cooked and sold her baked goods. She always saved a little money in a jar, and gave the money to the Lord. They loved the Lord, and were so thankful for their salvation.

He completed a course in Bible study which Bill provided for him, and Bill had the privilege of giving him a reward in church. The man was elated.

I had learned to do reflexology on the feet. It is an old Asian treatment which is still widely practiced in the Asian countries today. The principle is that all the nerves run into the feet. By carefully and properly messaging those nerve endings, it will improve circulation to areas and organs of the body. I still don't completely understand the practice, but I know it works on many illnesses. I have treated many people with good results.

I'll never forget my introduction to reflexology. My missionary friend, Sherry Daniels, lived in Nanyuki – about 130 miles from Nairobi. Sherry had frequent, painful flare-ups of an old back injury. One time it had gotten so painful she could barely sit. She came to Nairobi, and stayed with us while she was getting treatment.

I had been having a few issues, so Sherry asked, "LaMoin, will you go with me today when I take my treatment and let Kathy examine you?"

"I don't have any problems with my back, so how could she help me?"

"She treats many other things besides the back."

Sherry then explained to me what kind of treatments she was having – which were helping her. She explained the principle of reflexology to me.

"You've got to be kidding me! It sounds like witchcraft to me." I didn't want anything do with it. She wasn't about to touch my feet.

I finally agreed to go with Sherry to her treatment, but I wasn't going to leave the waiting room when I got there.

We arrived at a nice residence with a private treatment room in the back. We walked into a beautiful, clean waiting room. Soon a British woman came out and spoke to us. Sherry introduced me to Kathy, and told her I had driven her over for her treatment. They went into the treatment room while I waited in the only room that I was going to see.

After Sherry's treatment, she came out and lay down on a single bed. She told me the treatment made her tired, and she needed to rest for a short time before going home.

Kathy said to me, "Come on back while Sherry is resting, and I will just give you a free examination."

"No, thank you. I am not interested. There is nothing wrong with me. I don't need any treatments."

She was sweet and friendly, and she finally persuaded me to go back to the treatment room. She just wanted to show me what kind of treatments she practiced. I finally went back with her. The room was nice and white – like a doctor's treatment room. She wanted to just demonstrate the treatments to me.

I finally agreed, but I told her, "I don't believe in this at all. In fact, it sounds like witch craft to me." She laughed.

She sat on a small stool at my feet. She put my name on a small card with the outline of two feet on it – it reminded me of the cards we used in the dental office where I worked the year I graduated from high school. Well, she started pressing different points on my foot – and it hurt! Sometimes I felt like kicking her in the face! Each time she found a sore spot, she marked the area on that card.

At the end of the torture session, she told me everything which had been wrong with me in the past, and everything which presently bothered me! I was astounded! I couldn't believe it! She then explained the principles of reflexology and it made some sense to me. Later, Kathy taught me how to do reflexology. Real practitioners must be properly trained and licensed to give treatments, but I do it on friends and family.

This crippled man learned about my knowledge in this treatment. He asked me if I would do reflexology on him. He believed it would help him. Even though I know the treatment can help a lot of conditions, I told him I could not help him to walk. I did not want to raise his hopes of being cured. However, he pleaded with me to do it. I wanted to comfort him, and to let him know I was willing to give him my time.

I started to give him regular treatments. We prayed together that it would help him. To mine and Bill's complete surprise, strength came to the man's legs, and even though he could never walk normally, he was able to get out of his wheelchair. He would hold to furniture and walk a bit around the house. We assured him that it was God's work – not mine.

Bill ordered a copy of "The Jesus Film," and we got permission to go into one of the poorer Indian neighborhoods and show it. There were many apartment buildings with an open court yard in the middle of them. Bill bought a huge canvas which he tied up at one end of the courtyard area. People came to the area and sat, or they would stand on their balconies, and hundreds of them watched the film. Through that method, we got acquainted with some of them, and visited in their homes.

We were able to lead a few of them to Christ, but many heard the message of salvation.

We had to be patient when working with the Hindus and Muslims. We didn't see a lot of results. It is slow and can be discouraging. In our culture and in our Christian work, we are geared towards results and numbers. But, when working with the Indians, we had to try to be satisfied in knowing we were obeying God when He said, "Go into all the world and preach the gospel to every creature, baptizing them in the name of the Father, the Son, and the Holy Spirit" (Matthew 28:19,20). He didn't say we were to win all of them – but to "preach" to all of them. We cannot win them unless the Holy Spirit draws them to salvation, but we are commissioned to tell everyone about Christ, and to give them the opportunity to be saved - which we strived to do. We left the results in God's hands.

Yes, the work was slow, but we greatly rejoiced over even one of them coming to Christ. The Bible says there is rejoicing in the presence of the angels when one sinner is converted, (Luke 15:10). We rejoiced over the few who publically came to Christ.

Rose

I was in a jewelry store, and I met a pretty Indian woman who worked there. We got acquainted, and I invited her to come to church. She was Hindu, but she was divorced with a couple of sons and a small daughter. I will call her Rose. She was a bit of an outcast. She came to church, and we became friends. She, her teenage sons, and her young daughter all received Christ as their savior, and became faithful in church.

Later, we met a dentist who started coming to our home and to the church services. He was single, half Italian and half Afghan, and a Muslim by birth. When he saw Rose, he was surprised she was there. Later, he told us she was a prostitute.

Well, I don't know. He was in more of a position to know than we were. However, this I do know – she changed when she received Christ. Many scholars have written that our Lord was in the lineage of Rahab – who had been a prostitute. So, we didn't care what she "had" been, but what she had become. Praise God for her salvation!

Chapter 8
Motorcycles, Rain, and Cockroaches

Bill was trying to invent ways to win the Indian young people. We rode motorcycles in Kenya, and many of the young Indian men also rode motorcycles. Bill felt this was a good "hook," so he started riding with them. We did anything we could to make friends with them and to get them to church. He organized the "Capitol City Cycle Club." He planned short trips with the young Indian men to get closer to them in an effort to influence them to Christ. We usually had a variety of them in our home. Some of them wore turbans, some had beards, some had big bikes, some had small ones – but they all had a need of salvation.

They were a good group of young people. Our kids also rode motorcycles when they were home from school. They made good friends with many of the Indians. They liked to come to our home where there was a perpetual party. They were learning about America from us, and at the same time, we were learning about the Indians. Many came to the church, and some of them were saved.

Walking at Night in Lion Country

I never rode a motorcycle by myself, but I loved to ride with Bill. He and I rode a lot with Simon and Carol. They were faithful in church and our best friends. We had been in Nairobi a few months, and after the rainy season was over, we decided it would be fun to ride to Mombasa with them. Mombasa was on the coast and was about 300 miles from Nairobi. Simon and Carol took a few days off work, and we planned to leave on Monday morning. We could ride to Mombasa in about eight hours, so we would be there before dark.

Some plans just don't work out right – and neither did our plans to leave in the morning. One of the bikes had some problems, and the guys had to work on it. Well, you know how that goes! We finally left in the afternoon. We were determined to leave that day!

There were only about three places where we could buy gas – and a traveler in Kenya never passes up a gas station! We rode for about two and a half hours in the beautiful warm day until we came to Hunter's Lodge. We stopped to fill up the bikes with gas. While we were there, a car pulled in - coming from Mombasa, and going to Nairobi. The men got to talking, and the man in the car learned we were going to Mombasa.

He said, "It is raining hard on down the road. You'd better try not to ride any farther today, or you'll run into rain." Really? The rains were supposed to be finished.

After the man left, Bill and Simon said to Carol and me, "Maybe we'd better stay here tonight and go on in the morning."

Hunter's Lodge was an ideal place to stay. There was a small restaurant and rooms which were rustic, but okay. There was a river running past the rooms, and you could walk out on a little balcony and look out over the river and into the jungle. Typical Africa! They had a small zoo with several animals and birds. At any other time, I would have been delighted to stay there, but we had planned for weeks to go to Mombasa. We had already been delayed by the mechanical work on the bike, so now Carol and I wanted to go to Mombasa.

"No, let's go on to Mombasa. The big rains are finished, and it looks beautiful right now. Let's go on," we insisted. "We'll be okay."

The guys finally agreed, and we got on the bikes and started out. It was so wonderful with the wind on our faces and riding out through the open African wilderness. The road was a two lane, paved road, and there weren't many cars. We would meet a car once in a while, but it was pretty desolate.

Bill and I had never been to Mombasa, but had heard a lot about it. It was the vacation Mecca for the missionaries. I love to travel and to experience everything a country has to offer, so I was eager to go. It was even more exciting, because we were on the bikes. There is just something so refreshing and exhilarating about riding in the African bush on a motorcycle. I looked out over the grasslands, and saw herds of beautiful zebra, elephant, wilder beast, giraffe, and many species of deer. It was like a dream. I was energized!

There was one place to get gas between Hunter's Lodge and Tsavo. When we got to the next station, it was closed! We would have to ride to Tsavo before we could get food or gas again. We were a bit concerned. We thought, but prayed, that we would have enough gas. But, one thing was for certain – we did not want to run out of gas out in that wilderness which was lion country!

Tsavo is where 135 men were eaten by lions in less than one year in 1898 when they were building the Ugandan railroad between Mombasa and Nairobi There is a movie, "The Ghost and the Darkness," and a book, "The Man-eaters of Tsavo," that tells the gruesome story. These are true stories about how two unusually large lions started coming into the camp at night and dragging men from their tents and eating them. For months the lions outsmarted the hunters who tried to kill them. They seemed to have supernatural intelligence to know where the hunters were waiting, and then they would attack in another area. Patterson, the British engineer in charge of building the bridge for the railroad, finally killed the lions as he narrowly escaped being a victim. The lions were stuffed and are now in a museum in Chicago.

I told you that story to emphasize that we were riding through some pretty dangerous country. Soon, it got dark – and then it started to rain! It doesn't just rain in Kenya – it pours! We thought the rains were finished, so we didn't take any rain gear with us. We were riding through open, desolate lion country – at night and in the rain. No cars were on the road, because people do not travel at night in Kenya if they can prevent it. The darkness was so black we could barely see the road ahead of us. At any time, a large animal could have come across the road in front of us. We knew if that happened, it would do more than wreck our bike. We could see Simon's tail light, and I comforted myself with knowing if anything came into the road, he would hit it first. As long as I could see his tail light, I knew we were okay. Well sure, I was being selfish, but those were my thoughts – human preservation!

Simon and Carol were riding a Gold Wing which is a big bike – with a big gas tank. We were riding a 250 Honda with a much smaller gas tank. After we passed the gas station that was closed, we had good reason to be concerned. We rode on for a short time. Our bike began to slow down and then stop. Yep! We were out of gas – right in the middle of lion country. In the black African darkness! In the rain! We had a one liter (about a quart) can of gas with us. Bill poured the gas in the tank, and we rode on. We knew it couldn't last long.

We were cold, soaking wet, and no longer real excited when our bike stopped again. Simon came back to check on us. "I've already used my spare can of gas, and now we are completely out of gas," Bill said.

Motorcycles, Rain, and Cockroaches

"Well, my bike is out of gas too." Simon replied. "I don't know what we are going to do. There is nowhere close to get any. Tsavo is still about an hour away."

My eyes scanned the dark, rainy African wilderness, and then I saw a tiny, dim light about a half of a mile up ahead.

"Bill, look up there. There's a light. It must be a village. Maybe someone there will be able to help us."

"Even if it is a little village, they won't be able to help us. There's probably not a car or telephone within miles of this place." Thank you, Mr. Negative!! There were certainly no cars on the road for the night.

God said He would never leave us or forsake us – which means also in the wilderness of Africa! I guess we were just going to have to trust Him that the light up ahead was a village.

"Well," I said, "let's walk up there. At least, we will be closer to people if we have to sleep on the ground until daybreak." (Or we could be robbed and killed - I chose to think positive.)

Bill and Simon didn't have any alternate plans. We walked the bikes up the road toward the light – while we prayed! None of us felt comfortable. We knew at any moment, we could have been attacked by an animal. It was still pouring rain, and it was dark as coal. We were alert to our surroundings. At least, I wanted to see what was going to eat us!

We got closer to the light. We could now see it *was* a village. A village, meaning a few mud huts. We prayed harder. When we reached the light, we found a man there. God had answered our prayers. He was still taking care of us – even if we had been rather stupid in starting out in the rain at night.

The African man had a small hand operated pump with a small supply of gas which was kept to service any transport trucks which might need emergency gas while traveling through the area. We weren't in a truck – but we qualified as an emergency.

He filled our tanks, and we rode on. Maybe it was an angel outpost! I'm not kidding!

We finally reached Tsavo. There was a lodge, a restaurant, and a gas station – and they were all open. It was about ten o'clock at night, and the rain was still coming down in gulley washers.

We parked the bikes and went inside. We were tired, hungry, and needed the restroom. Our clothes and boots were dripping water as we went up the stairs to the restrooms. Carol and I pulled off our boots and poured the water out. Then we took off our clothes, and we literally wrung the water out of them. We put them back on and went downstairs. We had a good warm meal, relaxed, and looked around the lodge a bit.

The men said, "Why don't we just stay here for the rest of the night and go on to Mombasa in the morning?"

"No way," Carol and I argued. "We are already tired and wet, and after what we have endured, it can't get much worse. Let's just ride on to Mombasa."

Maybe we were in shock by then, and without the ability to exercise common sense. But we were challenged by this time. We walked outside, got on the bikes, filled them with gas, and continued on toward Mombasa. I know the few people who saw us thought we had surely lost our minds. A couple of British guys at the lodge couldn't believe we were going to ride to Mombasa – late at night and in the rain.

Yes, it was still raining when we arrived in Mombasa about two o'clock in the morning. We found the old hotel where we had booked reservations and checked in. The people at the desk looked at us as if we were crazy people. Maybe they had their own reservations about letting us stay in their hotel! We were sooooo tired! But we had won the victory – with no prize except the satisfaction that we could do it! We were so eager to get out of our wet clothing, and rest our tired bodies on a bed. If you've never ridden a motorcycle for ten hours through African wilderness in the cold rain, you have no idea what it can do to a body.

We gathered our small packs from the cycles, and trudged up the narrow, dark stairs to our rooms on the second floor. Simon and Carol's room was next door to ours. The rooms were old and badly furnished, but we didn't mind. They were inexpensive. All we needed was a bed. We quickly got out of our wet clothes, took a quick shower to wash the dirt off, put on dry clothes, and collapsed into bed. By then, it was about three-thirty in the morning.

At five o'clock, while we were in a dead sleep, we were suddenly awakened by loud, blood curdling, terrifying screaming! We jumped out of bed and ran outside on our small balcony. Simon was on his balcony next door.

"What is that screaming?" we asked.

"It's the Muslim call to prayer – over in that minaret," Simon answered, as he pointed over to the tall minaret which towered over some of the rooftops. "Beeal, (Bill) if I had a rifle, I would shoot him out of that tower."

While the Muslims were praying, we went back to sleep.

We stayed in Mombasa about three days. Simon and Carol showed us all around that important old sea port. It was a city with a history of slave trading, and they had a monument to mark the place of the slave markets. We saw a large bell which someone would ring to warn people the slave traders were coming. It was a grim reminder of so much suffering.

Mombasa was predominately Muslim; because of so many Arabs and Indians who controlled the economy there. It was interesting to see the Arabs serving coffee on the streets from a tall, brass coffee pot. The pot sat on a small pan with live coals to keep the coffee warm. A cup was hung on the side. When someone bought coffee, it was served from the cup. When the customer finished his coffee, the seller would wipe the cup with a dirty towel, and hang it back on the pot for the next customer. I have one of those pots in my family room today.

A Cockroach in the Chop Suey

We were eating in a small café one day, when Carol looked so disgusted and said, "That guy over there is eating his chicken like a hyena."

She was well trained in etiquette by her British father, and was often disgusted by the manners of others, or by bad food.

Later we went into a Chinese restaurant. Our food came, we asked the blessing, and Carol started to take the first bite.

"Oh, why me?" she groaned.

"What's wrong, Carol?"

"Look." She showed us a big cockroach in her food! We called the Chinese manager, and showed it to him.

"So sorry." He apologized, and quickly took the plate of food away. Soon he returned with another plate of food and said, "If you find another one, please let me know." We no longer felt hungry for Chinese food, so we left.

We said goodbye to hot and humid Mombasa, and headed back on the road for the long trip back to Nairobi. We did manage to leave early in the morning. After we rode for about an hour, it started raining. We rode all day in the rain. When we finally reached our home in Nairobi - which was one mile higher in altitude than Mombasa – we were tired, almost frozen to the bikes, and filthy. We were even dirtier than on our trip down the mountain, because there was more traffic on the roads, and all of the dirt and water was splashed up on us. But, we were able to buy gas, and we didn't fear being wrecked or eaten by an animal. Well, at least we thought we had a better chance in the daylight.

A Doctor's Visit

Simon came to the house with an American doctor, a pathologist from California. Dr. Siegel had his new BMW motorcycle flown from California to Kenya, so he could ride through Africa on his vacation. He had a problem with the bike, so he went to the Honda dealership, and met Simon. While he was there, one of the young Indians popped the clutch on the bike, and shattered it. Simon couldn't repair it, and there were no BMW clutches in Kenya to replace it. Simon told him he could make a clutch, but it would take more time than the doctor had before his flight back to America. He didn't want to ship the bike back home, because he still wanted to ride it around more of Africa. So he decided to leave it with us, let Simon fix it, and then return for it six months later.

When Dr. Siegel returned, the bike was as good as new, and he was grateful. He wanted Bill and me to ride to Mombasa with him to show him around. He said he would pay our expenses. We wanted to have more time to witness to that Jewish man, so we agreed to go with him. We traveled in style – resort hotels, expensive restaurants, and beautiful weather. I think God rewarded us with the trip, because of all we went through on the last one.

The doctor carried a little leather pouch with him which held his passport, tickets, money, and any other valuable documents. He was always forgetting it. I would see he left it behind, and I would pick it up and return it to him. I suppose he had been spoiled to having a nurse right by his side while he performed operations. He didn't have to remember much, or do much for himself.

He left the pouch on the dinner table one night, and I picked it up and gave it to him.

I said, "I would hate for you to operate on me, because you would probably leave a sponge or instrument in me."

He replied, "Oh, the people I operate on wouldn't know the difference." He performed autopsies.

Bill said, "Yeah, you doctors can bury your mistakes, but we preachers have to live with ours."

When we returned from Mombasa, we took a trip up to RVA. We wanted to show him the school and the beautiful Rift Valley. When we got higher into the mountains, it was cold. By the time we arrived back home, we were almost frozen to the bikes. Bill could hardly move his fingers on the handle grips. I was wearing a helmet with goggles. When I removed the goggles, my face was covered in dirt with white circles around my eyes. I looked like a raccoon. I went inside, ran a tub of hot water, and soaked until I had feeling back in my body.

We witnessed to Dr. Siegel many times during the days he was with us in Nairobi. We were never able to get him to see the truth about Jesus being the Messiah, but we fulfilled our responsibility to tell him the gospel. We lost contact with him after awhile, but if he never got saved, at least he will have no excuse when he stands before God at the Great White Throne Judgment.

Chapter 9
Collecting Elephant Dung on Mt. Elgon

We were happy in Nairobi, and had settled into the ministry with the Indians and with daily living. We devoted most of our time to trying to reach the Indian community with the gospel. Mary was a wonderful help to me in the house, and she even did a lot of the cooking while I was teaching or visiting.

We tried to go to visit the kids at RVA as often as we could. Sometimes we would drive up on Saturday and spend the day with them. About once a month, they would ride the bus into town on Saturday and spend the day. We would usually take them back to school so they could spend more time at home. Sometimes Greg came in alone, and Bill would take him back to RVA on the bike. I never really rested until he returned home. The roads were rough, steep, and dangerous. There were also bandits who worked on the road. He would wait as late as possible to return Greg to RVA, and then he would have to ride back after dark. But we loved the kids, and we wanted them with us as much as possible.

Everyone needs to get away from the daily responsibilities occasionally, and we did get out of Nairobi a few times. After language school, the Camps went to a station in Kitale, which was near to the Ugandan border. They invited us to come up to spend a few days with them. We needed a break, so we accepted their invitation.

The distance between Nairobi and Kitale is about two hundred miles, and it takes about six hours to drive it – depending on how many people and animals are in the road. Nairobi is approximately 5,889 miles above sea level. We drove even higher into the mountains on the way to Kitale. The steep, winding road was in disrepair in many places which made it even more dangerous. There were no guard rails along the thirty mile long escarpment which overlooked the Great Rift Valley. The valley floor is about 1,800 feet above sea level, while the height of the crest is about 6,900 feet. It was breathtaking – in beauty and apprehension!

Sometimes the lories (trucks) would be driving so slowly we had to pass them – even on curves – and just pray nothing was coming from the opposite direction. One time Bill passed a truck, and just when we were overtaking it – with a great view down over the escarpment – another big truck came toward us. No one panicked. Both truck drivers got over as far as they could and we went through the middle. TIK.

Some missionaries were on their way to RVA for the graduation of their children, when their car went over the escarpment, and they plunged thousands of feet below to their deaths. Another couple was robbed on that road. Those are some of the perils of missionary service.

I think if I lived in Africa for the rest of my life, I would never get over the excitement of seeing all the animals roaming freely over the land. We get so excited here in America when we see a couple of deer, but in Kenya it was common to drive along and see herds of gazelle, Cape buffalo, wildebeest, zebra, giraffe, and other animals you see only in a zoo here.

I was fascinated by the giraffes. Kenya has the largest population of giraffes in the world – about 45,000, which is one-third of the population of the world. A male giraffe is about 18 – 20 feet tall and weighs around 4,300 pounds. They were so huge, yet so graceful. They ran as if they were floating. They have a tongue about 18 inches long, and it is used to grasp leaves and twigs. Their tongues are tough enough to allow them to eat the thorny twigs from the thorn trees. They can munch on the tops of the trees where other animals cannot reach. There is an antiseptic in their saliva which takes care of any wounds from the thorns. Isn't God's creation amazing? The adult giraffes need to eat about 65 pounds of vegetation a day. They spend 15- 20 hours a day eating. They require little sleep – 20 minutes to 2 hours a day! They must get down on their front knees to drink, so it makes them easy prey for lions. Remarkable animals!

We had to stop a couple of times for giraffes to cross the road. We stopped to watch some of them grazing at the side of the road. Bill got so close to one to take a picture that he could have walked under him. God was kind and didn't let the giraffe kick his head off.

We saw many of the ugly, nasty looking Cape buffalo. They are dangerous animals, so it isn't wise to get close to them. Well, it isn't wise to get too close to any of the animals, since they are wild! The buffaloes usually have long, thick saliva (Bill would say "snot") hanging from their noses and mouths, while exercising their bodily functions.

The buffalo is the mascot for RVA, so every time Wyvonna would see them, she'd remark, "And that is what represents us." TIK.

We drove past Lake Nakuru which is home to thousands, sometimes millions, of fuchsia pink flamingoes. It is quite a spectacular sight! The whole lake looks pink. Only in Africa!

We enjoyed the trip, and finally arrived at the Camp's home in Kitale. We had not seen them for a few months, and we had a lot of catching up to do. They had settled into their work there in the small town and were content. Cheryl was a teacher, so she was home schooling Matthew and Lauren.

After a couple of days of good fellowship, and lots of Cheryl's great cooking, we decided to take a trip to Mt. Elgon – the second highest mountain in Kenya. It separates Kenya from Uganda, and it is about four hours from Kampala.

The Camps, Bill, and I piled into their Peugeot car, and headed for the mountain. Just before getting in the car, Cheryl grabbed a couple of burlap bags, and put them in the trunk. We traveled a short distance, and arrived at the Mt. Elgon National Park. We paid a small fee to enter, and then drove along the narrow trails - far into the thick jungles.

We knew there were many herds of elephants which lived in the area, and we were hoping to see some of them. Carroll drove slowly, and we looked closely into the thick jungle to try to spot the elephants. I was flabbergasted to learn that 10,000 pound elephants can successfully hide from view among the trees. But, it's true! That's why we had to search for them. We knew they were there, because we saw droppings along the road.

We were barely moving along the narrow jungle road. Suddenly, a herd started across the road a few yards in front of the car. A big bull was leading them, and there were females and babies following him. The little ones were so cute.

Cheryl and I said to Carroll, "Get a little closer, so we can have a better look at them."

"I don't think I should."

"Oh, come on. Quickly! They're going into the jungle."

Carroll had stopped, so he put the car in gear and started driving slowing toward them. The big bull had crossed the road first and stopped, while the others were crossing. He saw us moving toward them. All of a sudden he started to paw the ground. Quickly he flapped his ears, screamed, and started toward the car. The kids were screaming, and Carroll was trying to get the car in reverse. We were scared! My heart was pounding.

We were all yelling at Carroll, "Back up, back up!" Within seconds – which seemed like minutes – the car started back. The elephant stopped abruptly when he saw us going back. He was just protecting the herd and giving us a warning.

We drove out of the dense jungle area onto a plateau. I then realized why Cheryl had put the burlap bags into the car.

"I brought some bags to pick up some of this elephant dung for fertilizer. I'll bet it would be great for plants."

"How are we going to get it?" I asked.

"We will just pick up the dry piles. It's rather like straw."

As Carroll drove around over the mountain, one of us would yell, "Stop the car. There are some piles."

Then we would jump out, scoop up the dung, and put it in the bags which each of us had. We walked a lot, and picked up lots of piles of dung. We learned some of it wasn't completely dry when we picked it up. You can guess the rest.

We laughed and laughed as we ran around over that mountain collecting elephant dung. The men couldn't believe it! We were having fun. We filled our bags about half full, and felt quite accomplished as we put them in the trunk. I took mine home, put it on my plants, and killed every one of them. Elephant dung is strong! TIK.

We then went to Kitum Cave on the slopes of Mt. Elgon. Most people go with a guide, who usually carries an automatic weapon. We had no guide – and no gun. *What's the big deal?* Well, this is the only place in the world where elephants are known to go underground. They go into the cave, and scrape the walls for the salt which the rocks contain. It is also used by leopards, hyenas, Cape buffaloes, and other animals.

Yes, we were a bit crazy, I guess. We had heard a lot about it, so we wanted to see it. We climbed up a rugged slope and went inside. After we entered, we were in a large open area where we saw evidence of where the animals had been, but didn't see any. Of course, we didn't go back into the other areas of the cave. I have heard that Kitum Cave is less stable than most caves, and cave-ins are more likely because of the mining of the elephants. We just stayed in the opening room where there were thousands of bats, which was a bit risky, because bats do carry rabies. Some people have been bitten by them and contracted rabies.

We have taken so many dumb chances. Any kind of a ferocious, hungry animal could have been hiding in that cave. Isn't it wonderful how our heavenly Father takes care of us when we don't have sense enough to realize danger? Maybe an animal was watching us, and getting prepared to attack, and our guardian angel stood between us. Our angels don't have time to camp around about us – we are always keeping them busy. No kidding, I fully believe those angels have protected our lives so many times. We should not knowingly put ourselves in situations and tempt God, but He knows how ignorant we are sometimes, so our angel just shakes his head, and says, "Here we go again."

Kitum Cave was later featured in the book, "The Hot Zone" which described Ebola – a deadly disease which begins with a headache and fever, and then the internal organs begin to dissolve and liquefy. The patient bleeds from every orifice of the body, and death comes within about 24 hours. The mortality rate is 100%. There is no cure! To my knowledge, two people died of this disease in the Nairobi Hospital. Later the cave was thoroughly examined by scientists, because they believed the disease originated there. Of course, we didn't have all of this information at that time. Thank you again - my beautiful angel and my heavenly Father.

Chapter 10
A Vacation from Hell

The kids came home for a school break, and we decided to take them to Mombasa. We always tried to have some family fun when they were home. We didn't have a lot of money for the nice tourist hotels along the beautiful coast of Mombasa, so we made reservations to stay at CPK (a Christian guesthouse). We had never been there before, but had heard about it from other missionaries. This compound was old, but we would be among other Christians, and the price was affordable for us. There were some newer units, but they were already reserved, so we thought one of the old cottages would be okay.

We arrived in the middle of the afternoon. After registering, the attendants gave us a quick tour of the compound. It was quite large, and had the office with an adjoining community dining room where all the guests had meals together. We walked around, and saw the newer cottages. They even had a proper roof on them! The older ones had thatched roofs. We determined to make earlier reservations next time and get a newer unit.

We took the key to our cottage, unlocked the door and went in. There was one large room with three single beds on the right. On the left was a small area with one double bed, and was separated by a partition on half of the room. At the end of the large room to the left, was a short, narrow hall which led to the bathroom. All the beds were covered by mosquito nets, hanging from a hook in the ceiling and draped down over the beds.

We needed the mosquito nets, because this was at the coast where malaria was rampant. Our American Consular in Mombasa (who was an acquaintance of mine) contracted malaria, quickly went into a coma, and died.

I was a bit surprised there were no screens or glass in the window behind the beds. Round, iron bars had been installed for security, and simple cotton curtains covered it - except for about a foot at the top. We looked up into the thatched roof and saw thousands of mosquitoes! Mosquitoes love my blood! If there is one within a mile, he will find me. I also have a bit of an allergy to the bites.

I said, "Bill, we can't stay in here with all of these mosquitoes. They will eat us alive, or carry us away to share with their relatives. And how many of them will infect us with malaria?"

"You're right, but we'll put some mosquito coils in here to drive them out. By the time we get back from town, they should be gone."

We got the coils from the office, and lit about four of them. A mosquito coil is some kind of a hard substance which is coiled like the burner on an electric stove. It sits on a little metal stand, and you light it at one end. The flame goes out, and it leaves a live, smothering fire which sends off a smoke with insecticide in it which kills mosquitoes or drives them out.

After we unpacked the car, we headed into town to show the kids around. We just drove around town, and then stopped at some of the little kiosks to look at souvenirs. We drove along the coast, and saw the beautiful tourist hotels. Some missionaries could afford to stay in those hotels, but we didn't have the money. It was getting late, so we headed back to the cottage.

When we got back, we went into the dining room for dinner. The tables were nicely set with tablecloths. At each plate, there was a cloth napkin in a wooden napkin ring with a hand carved animal on top. Nice – except for the fact we were instructed to fold up the napkin and place it back in the ring after each meal. Those napkins were used for a week before they were changed, or until the guest left. We had to remember which animal we had, because that marked our seats. I had no problem remembering. I didn't want to use someone else's napkin! We had a nice dinner, met some other guests, and then went to our room for the evening.

When we walked into the room, we checked for mosquitoes, and they were gone! However, there were big red safari ants in the room. Wyvonna and Greg are allergic to insect bites and stings, so the ants were totally unacceptable! We went to the office and got some insect spray, and finally were able to kill all the ants. The kids were a bit apprehensive about the place, but we assured them everything was fine, and to get a good night's rest, because we had a big day coming up tomorrow.

Greg took the bed closer to the door, Shaleen was in the middle bed, and Wyvonna had the bed at the far end of the room. Bill and I slept in the bed behind the partition. We settled into bed, under our nets, and drifted off to sleep.

I was sleeping soundly, when suddenly; I was awakened by a piercing scream from one of the girls. Bill and I jumped up, and ran to see what had happened.

Wyvonna had jumped out of her bed, escaping strangulation by the mosquito net, and was standing by her bed with a terrorized expression.

"What's wrong?" I asked - after I was able to breathe.

"There was a rat in my bed."

"Oh, honey, you must have had a nightmare."

"Well then, it was the most real nightmare I've ever had. No, there was a rat in my bed. I felt his little paws at my side, and when I moved, he ran down to my feet."

Mind you this all happened quickly, and during the panic, Bill turned on the light. When the light came on, we saw the rat run along the baseboard, up the wall, and out of the window. He was gigantic! We finally got the three of them back into their beds and under the nets.

"Okay, the rat is gone now. Everything is okay. So try to go to sleep."

Bill and I went back to bed. I was having a hard time going to sleep myself. The girls were nervous.

Finally, they asked, "Can we leave this small light on?"

"Yes, leave it on."

I had just gotten into a dead sleep, and I heard both the girls screaming. Again, we jumped up, and went to check on them. I guess it's somewhat of a miracle we didn't get tangled up in those mosquito nets and hang ourselves.

"What's wrong now? We asked.

"Something flew in the window," they both yelled.

"It's just a bird," Greg said. He was a bit disgusted with his sisters.

It flew down the little hall toward the bathroom, and when it flew back towards the beds, they started screaming, "It's a bat!" And it was a bat!

I said, "Just stay under the nets and it can't get to you."

In the meantime, Bill and Greg each grabbed a shoe, and were trying to hit it. The bat would fly around the room – with the girls screaming – and then back towards the bathroom. Every time it flew towards the beds, the girls started screaming, and Bill and Greg would strike at it with their shoes.

Soon there was a knock at the door. I opened it, and it was the African night watchman.

He asked, "What is going on? Are you fighting?" He naturally heard the screaming, and at the top of the curtain, he could see the guys hitting at the bat. He came to the logical conclusion there was a big fight going on.

"Yes," I replied, "We are fighting a bat. Would you like to come in and help?"

He then smiled as if this was an everyday occurrence. "He will go outside." He stepped back to a tree, broke off a good limb, and came inside. Bill and Greg were still chasing the bat, and the girls were still screaming when he flew near. It was now about two o'clock in the morning.

The watchman started chasing the bat. By then, I was almost feeling sorry for the bat. The poor thing was scared out of his wits. Now the watchman was swinging at him with the limb. Each time he tried to hit him, we heard "swish," and the leaves would fly in every direction. The floor was covered with leaves. It was extremely hot and humid in Mombasa, and we didn't have air conditioning. The poor watchman was sweating and exhausted. He wiped his brow and said, "I will kill this one." He finally hit the bat, knocked it to the floor, and kicked it outside. TIK.

After all of the excitement was over, we again got into our beds to try to sleep. The light stayed on, the girls stayed awake, and soon I heard, "What if a snake crawls through the window?"

"Oh, snakes can't climb," Greg said.

Well, I certainly wasn't going to correct him on that one. But I knew better. A huge cobra had climbed through the open window of a missionary friend's bedroom window when they were asleep one night. The window was by the dresser, and when the snake came through the window, it knocked a glass vase off the dresser and alerted Joel. He killed it. But that was not the time or place for that story!

When morning came, we dragged our tired, sleepless bodies to the dining room for breakfast. I was sure we had disturbed and frightened everyone on the compound. Now we had to face them. Although, I was a bit annoyed with everyone. We could have been the victims of a horrific murder scene, but no one had come to check on us. Anyway, I slithered to our table, and tried to not be seen.

As soon as we were seated, one Scandinavian just had to ask, "What happened last night? I was awakened to what seemed like a hundred girls screaming?" *Yeah, thanks a lot for your concern.* TIK. No place like Africa!

Did we remain there for the rest of the holiday? Now, what do you think? Of course not! We bit the financial bullet, and went to a better hotel!

Tsavo

Another time when the kids were home, we took a trip to the Tsavo Game Park. The game parks – or reserves – are huge areas of land where the animals roam freely, and that space has been dedicated to them. It is not open for development in any other way. Tsavo is the largest national park in Kenya, and you can see the "Big 5" – Masai lion, black rhino, Cape buffalo, elephant, and leopard. There were also giraffe, zebra, and many other animals. Tsavo also has the largest herds of elephants than any other park. They are usually covered with the red dust of the area. They like to go into the streams and cool off, and then when they come out, they will suck the dust into their trunks, and blow it all over them. Remember - this is also the area where the lions ate the railroad workers.

We called and reserved a cabin in the park, and we hoped it would be a more pleasant experience than our cottage in Mombasa. We turned off the main road between Nairobi and

Mombasa, and drove along a dirt road for a few miles. We finally reached the area of the cabins, where there was also a nice lodge. We checked in at the office, and found our cabin. We parked, got out, and were welcomed by several monkeys. They ran up and grabbed onto our legs, looking for food or anything they could steal. Then they climbed up on the kids, and reached into their pockets to find something to eat. We were warned they would come into the cabin if a door or window was left open, and they would steal anything in sight. They were cute and fun, but they were also a nuisance.

We found the cabin to be similar to the one in Mombasa. It was certainly no Holiday Inn. It had one large room with three beds; one smaller room with two twin beds (located just off the porch), a crude bathroom, and a small, open kitchen area in the back were we could cook over an open fire. It was plain with all the "African charm." The girls wanted the small room off the porch, and Greg slept in our large room.

We unloaded all of our gear, and then went for a sightseeing ride. We just drove along trails. There were no roads. It was wilderness. It didn't take long to see all kinds of animals. A herd of elephants was crossing in front of us, so Bill stopped. There was one baby that was only about three feet high. He saw our car, turned toward it, screamed, and acted like he was going to charge us. The mama started pushing him in the behind with her trunk, and pushed him on across the trail. It was the cutest thing. He was doing what came naturally.

After we went to bed, we could hear the sounds of different animals. After all, we were in a wild place. After a short time, the girls started knocking on our door. They were frightened and no longer wanted the independence of the little room off the porch. It was a bit frightening, because the animals roamed around the cabins at night. We moved their beds into our large room.

The next day we were driving around, and I saw a clump of bushes.

"Bill, drive through that trail in those bushes, and let's see what is on the other side."

"No, I am not going to take a chance on going in there."

"Well, why not? You can see tracts where other vehicles have gone through there." I suppose that many times, my desire for adventure outweighs my common sense. It's a good thing I have a guardian angel – and a sensible husband.

"Yes, but we don't have four-wheel drive. We could get stuck in there. This area is too isolated and wild to take a chance. If we did get stuck, we wouldn't dare get out and walk for help. No, forget it. I'm not driving in there."

All of my persuasion wouldn't budge him. Being cautious is so boring! We drove on into other areas, and saw many animals. It was great. We did see the "Big 5" along with others. We had been warned to be back at the cabins before dark. It was getting late, so we reluctantly headed back.

After we got back to the cabin area, we were talking to another guest. He asked us where we had been driving, and Bill told him.

"Did you see that big boa constrictor out there?"

"No, where was it?"

He started to describe the area. "There was a clump of bushes with a little trail going through them. It looked a little risky, but once I got through the bushes, there was a large open area. Right there in that open area, a huge boa was swallowing a gazelle. We just sat and watched it for awhile. The gazelle was about half way into his mouth, and he was taking his time and swallowing slowly."

"That is where I tried to get you to go!" I said to Bill.

The man said, "Well, I have been told that once the snake swallows an animal, they will not move for a couple of days until they digest the meal. It might still be there tomorrow."

Early the next morning, we headed back there. We drove through the bushes and saw the large, open area, but no snake. I was so disappointed! Now, why would I even want to see such a repulsive sight? Well – it would have been different and something that I will never have the opportunity to see again. Besides – it's a great missionary snake story!

Chapter 11

The Night Train to Mombasa

I will never forget riding the train from Nairobi to Mombasa. We had heard a lot about the train, so we decided we had to try it. We had a few free days, so we bought tickets, and headed for the station. We arrived a few minutes late, and then learned our tickets were for a car which was almost at the end of the train. We started running down the wooden platform next to the tracks. In our rush, I didn't notice a hose which was lying across the platform. I'm still not quite sure how it happened, but that hose ended up in the toe of my sandals, and I ended up face down on the platform! It was a great way to start a vacation. TIK. I gathered up my injured pride, and we stepped into the train. We found our seats which were in a closed cabin. The seats pulled out for beds at night. Oh, yes, we were going to spend the night on this famous train.

The train was an old model – made in Britain, probably around the time the railroad was build. The days of grandeur were past, and the train should have passed with the era. The walkways between the windows and the cabins were narrow, and the lights didn't work at night. We could lock our cabin from the inside, but not from the outside, so when we both left the cabin to go to the dining car, we didn't leave any valuables inside.

The dining car was quaint, and reflected the grand style of years gone by. There were still white table linens which were a bit worn. The china and cutlery had seen better days - it was bent and chipped. However, the antiquity was a pleasant part of the whole experience. Two meals were served – at 6:00 and 8:00 – so they could accommodate all of the passengers. We were advised to eat at 6:00, because the dishes weren't completely clean at the 8:00 meal. We made sure we were there at 6:00.

They had small restrooms, but most of the time, the flush toilets didn't work. When that happened, we had no choice but to use the national type of toilets which were also available – a hole in the floor. It took a bit of practice and a strong body to be able to use these "squatting" toilets, but we managed.

After dinner, we walked through the train, and found our cabin. We locked the door, and prepared our beds for the night. All of the linens and pillows were furnished. They, too, were a bit well used, but adequate. We had a small sink in the cabin, so we washed up, and lay down to try to sleep. It was a good thought! However, this train was so slow, and it stopped numerous times throughout the night. Each time it stopped, it lurched and made loud screeching sounds. Sleep was impossible. If I could have seen anything out the window, it wouldn't have been so bad, but it was too black outside. If it had not been for wanting the experience of sleeping overnight, it would have been better to take the day train – which we did on our return trip.

It usually took about six hours to drive to Mombasa. After about seventeen hours, this train rolled into the Mombasa depot. In spite of everything, we actually enjoyed the experience.

We Celebrated our 25th Wedding Anniversary in a Cave

Have you ever thought of dining in a cave, stalactites looking down on you, and surrounded by walls embedded with fossil shells? Doesn't that sound exciting? Well, I was excited about it, when we went to Ali Barbour's Cave. No, it wasn't the real hideout of the fictitious Ali Baba, but it was named in thought of the famous tale. A man named George Barbour had the bright idea of starting a classy restaurant in these caves in Diani Beach, a few miles from Mombasa. George's family name was Barbour, so he named the restaurant "Ali Barbour's Cave Restaurant."

These caves were formed in coral limestone thousands of years ago, and gradually modified by tidal action. The entrance to the cave complex was a drink area, covered with palm tree branches for a roof, which was supported by a gum tree. From this point, we walked down stone steps, which were cut from the rock, to two lower dining areas about ten meters below ground. The top was open to the African starry night sky. There was a sliding roof in case of rain. The interior of those caves carried cleverly hidden lights along its wall, creating a truly romantic aura. The menu was international, but the specialty was seafood.

We were in a cave, but the interior decoration and atmosphere were enchanting! The round tables were adorned with white linen table cloths with a blue trim, white linen napkins, silverware, crystal, and a candle. The stars overhead, the soft dinner music from the speakers - installed in the walls of the cave - and the candlelight completed the ambiance of the room.

As we enjoyed a scrumptious seafood meal, I felt transported into some imaginary setting in the world of the rich – until suddenly there was a bit of a chaotic stirring on the other side, and we saw a mongoose (an animal about four feet long with a long face, small rounded ears, short legs and a long tapering tail) run around the walls and up the stairs. I awoke from my trance and realized I was still in Africa. TIK.

Chapter 12
They Cut His Throat

There were many dangers in Kenya which required diligence and prayer, but one of the most dangerous was home robberies. Each house was enclosed by a high fence and gate. Most people had guard dogs and/or watchmen to guard the property by day and night. We didn't like to clean up after dogs, nor did we like the responsibility of caring for them. Please forgive me, all of you animal lovers, but I can't think of many things which are less tasteful than walking around scooping up dog poop! Anyway, dogs could easily be distracted by someone giving them food, or they can be killed by poisoned food. So, we choose not to have dogs on the property. We did have a watchman for a long time, but realized the robbers would either kill him, or get his cooperation by dividing the loot with him. We finally decided to live by the scripture in (Psalm 127:1), "….except the Lord keep the city, the watchman waketh but in vain." Most of the time the watchman would not even wake up! TIK.

The Lord also knew that most of the watchmen would be sleeping when they should be watching. When we did have a watchman, we came home many times to find him in such a sound sleep that he didn't hear us come in. We sometimes played tricks on him to let him know we had caught him sleeping, but we still couldn't break him of the habit. If we could walk all around him and take things, certainly any robbers could easily eliminate him.

The robbers did not come alone, but with a gang of ten to fifteen men. They would come in the middle of the night when everyone was sleeping. Sometimes they would put a sleeping gas in the house to be sure the occupants remained asleep. But usually they just stormed the house, and used large sledge hammers to knock the doors down.

Bill rigged an alarm with the siren from an old fire truck. He had a transformer made which transformed the 220V down to a 6Volt system. It measured about two feet by two feet. He put a switch on top of it, so we could just flip the switch, and the siren would go off. It was like a fire engine in the house. It would have frightened away any robbers - and also awaken all the neighbors.

One night we were in a deep sleep, and suddenly we both jumped straight up in the bed. There was a loud noise at the window. It sounded like someone had hit it with a heavy object. I just knew our time had come!

"Did you hear that noise?" I whispered to Bill.

"Yes."

Then another loud noise was at our bedroom door, which opened to the back yard. Then our outside motion lights came on. I froze! But no door came down. Bill looked out the window, but didn't see anything. Then he said, "I'm going to check outside. Get your hand on that switch, and be ready to pull it." Oh, sure – about the same time they killed him, and cut my hand off!

I was almost paralyzed. I don't know if I could have even pulled the switch, but I got ready. Bill went upstairs to the balcony and looked, but he couldn't see anyone outside. Then everything was quite. We didn't hear any more noise. We never knew what had hit our window and door. Maybe it was a person, and when the bright light came on, he ran. We never knew, but it certainly scared us, and we thanked God for protecting us.

Some of our missionary friends were not so blessed. One missionary family was robbed late at night by thirteen men who invaded the house and broke down every door outside and inside. Richard had such poor eyesight that he couldn't see anything without his glasses. The robbers made him and his wife and their two children assemble in the living room while they ransacked the house. They pulled out all the drawers, dumped the contents on the floor, and took anything of value.

Darlene had a set of beautiful diamond wedding rings she had never removed since they were married. One of the men saw them, and demanded she remove them. She tried, but they would not come off. He drew back his panga - a knife about three feet long with a four inch wide blade.

He said, "Get them off or I will cut your hand off." Naturally she was terrified. "Please let me go to put some lotion on, so I can get them off." He finally permitted her to go with another man for the lotion. That helped to slip them off, and he took them.

After being in the house for about four hours, they put all of their loot into the bed sheets, and tied them up. They demanded the keys to the car. The men had not given Richard time to put his glasses on when they came into the house.

"Please, let me go get my glasses, so I can find the keys." They didn't believe him, and one of the guys hit him across the head with the flat side of his panga, and knocked him down. Darlene then begged them to let him get his glasses. They finally told her to go get them while they guarded him. She got his glasses, and he found the keys. Then the guys loaded all of their stolen items into Richard's car.

In the meantime, one of them was eyeing their fourteen year old daughter. "How old is she?" he asked Darlene.

"Twelve," she answered.

"She looks older than twelve."

"No, she *is* twelve. She's tall for her age."

Then she heard them arguing. The one man wanted to take her with them. In fact, he had set his mind on it. Another man told him she was too young. They argued for awhile over it, but God just intervened, and the first man was persuaded to leave her.

When the robbers finally left the house, (in Richard's car) they used ropes and tied Richard, Darlene, and the girls – hands and feet – and put blankets over their heads. Darlene's ropes were not tied as securely as Richard's, and she managed to get her hands loose. The blanket was already shutting off their air. She was beginning to gasp for breath when she freed herself, and then she freed Richard and the children. They notified the police, but of course, the men were never caught. TIK. The police were only good at giving tickets for parking violations.

Our Indian Friends Were Robbed

Sunil was a young Indian man who was in the cycle club. He had received Christ and attended our church. One night a group of men broke into his home that he shared with his parents. They were beating his father, and Sunil tried to defend him. One man hit Sunil in the face with the sharp edge of his panga, and cut a big gash from his temple down along his cheek. They took all the valuables they could find and fled. The police and friends were called, and they got the family to the hospital, but the robbers were never found. Sunil wore a terrible scar in memory of that night.

One night a group of men went to a house just down the street from us. The watchman gave resistance, and they promptly sliced his throat with a panga, and left him dead while they proceeded to rob the house, and terrify the occupants.

The guard was honest, refused to cooperate, and met his death. That is the reason we decided not to employ a guard. We didn't want anyone to die over the few material things in our house. In other cases, the guards were in cahoots with the bad men. The guard would inform them of your movements and routine. It was then easy for them to know when the best time was to rob the house. Why pay a guard for helping them?

Robberies in the City

It was not safe to wear good jewelry, and many women had been robbed in Nairobi. One day I was having lunch with one of my friends, whose husband worked at the American Embassy. She was wearing a turtle neck, and I thought it was a bit odd to wear a turtle neck in the warm weather.

"Why are you wearing a turtle neck? Aren't you hot?"

She pulled down the neck to reveal what looked like a recent surgical scar around her throat. "What happened to you? Did you have surgery?"

"No, I was driving downtown, and had to stop for a traffic light. It was hot, so I rolled my window down. A man was walking past the car. He looked at me, and he noticed my heavy gold chain around my neck. He reached in the window and grabbed it, and tried to break the chain. But the chain was doubled and would not break. He had the chain in his hand, and was pulling and snapping it to break it. I couldn't even scream because the chain was cutting off my breath. I was so frightened. I thought he was going to choke me to death. I was hoping the chain would break, so I could breathe again. The light changed, and the cars were trying to go, so he finally released the chain and ran. I sat there for a few minutes trying to get my breath before I could even drive. It cut my neck, and it is just now healing." TIK.

In the Indian culture the women have a lot of gold jewelry. When they get married, their friends and family give them gold jewelry for wedding gifts. We attended several Indian weddings in Nairobi. I was always amazed – yes, and a little envious – as the people passed through the receiving line. Each one placed on the bride a gold necklace, bracelet, ring, broach, or gave her earrings. And, this was almost pure gold – 22k! The bride would have gold bracelets up to her elbows on both arms, numerous necklaces around her neck, several rings on each finger, and broaches pinned on her. The gold weighed so much, it actually looked uncomfortable.

One Indian lady was walking down the street with several gold bangles on her arm. A man walked up beside her, whacked off her arm with a panga, put the arm in a shopping basket, then ran and boarded a bus. Another passenger saw blood dripping from the basket. He told the driver, who drove to the nearest police station. The police found the arm – with the gold bangles on it – in the shopping basket. TIK.

We never left any valuables in the car, because they would not be there when we returned. We also had to be astute when we were in the car. Many times, the driver would be told he/she had a flat tire or that something was wrong with the car. When the driver got out to check the car, they would open the door and steal from the car.

Sometimes, someone would come to the driver's side and distract him, while his partner reached into the car on the other side, and grabbed a briefcase or whatever was available. They had many different methods to rip you off. We just had to constantly be mindful of their tricks. Recently, a missionary friend in Kenya had his briefcase and computer stolen from his car.

Dinner with the Camps

Kiambogo at RVA

Language School — Brackenhurst

Mary

I am picking up elephant dung!

Our 25th Wedding Anniversary in Ali Barbour's Cave Restaurant

Wyvonna, Shaleen, and friend

Some Indian church members

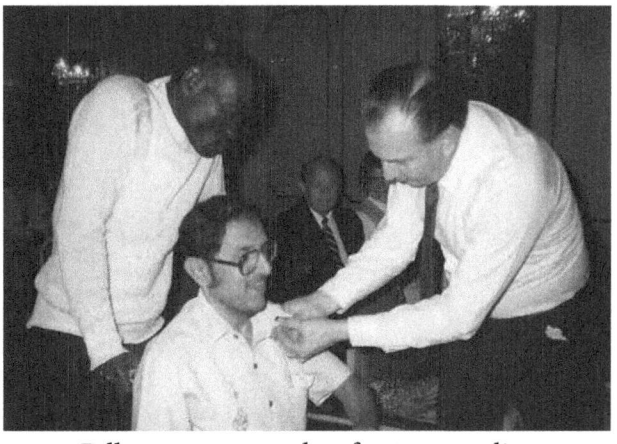

Bill presents award to former muslim

Our church at the Sarit Center

An open market

Mombasa

Our family: Shaleen, LaMoin, Bill, Greg, and Wyvonna

A Matatu

The ostrich hatching babies

My English class

Some members of the Capitol City Cycle Club

The American Embassy

Results of Bill's boating accident

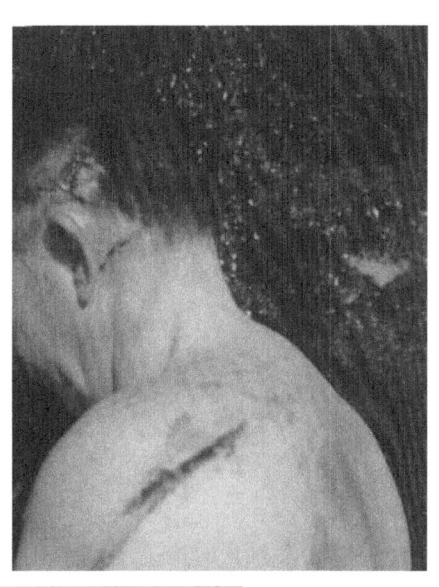

Bill standing by an ant hill

The Sarit Center

Chapter 13
My Key Frustration

"What is your greatest frustration on the field?" This is a question most missionaries are asked many times during furlough. We wives usually have similar answers: culture, customs, driving, language, rearing children on a foreign field, food, and on and on. However, one of my greatest frustrations was KEYS!

"Keys?" I can hear you ask.

"Yes, Keys!"

Have you ever thought much about keys? I'll bet you haven't. Keys are a source of security. We think when we lock our doors; it will keep the thieves out. We lock our cars, thinking it will keep them from being stolen. Banks keep locked safes to secure money. The list is endless. We feel secure after we lock the doors, and we have the important little gadget called a "key" to further enhance our good feeling that all is well. If you only have two house keys and a set of car keys to keep you comfortable, then you probably look upon the key as a great blessing and sense of security – especially the teenagers love those treasured car keys. However, I consider that little object called "the key" as a great source of frustration!

In Kenya, as in most third world countries, we had to be careful to keep everything locked, if we expected it to be in its place when we wanted it. Things just had a habit of disappearing. TIK. In the African culture, everyone had house help (help?).

Labor was extremely cheap, and it provided work for the Africans. But sometimes they just could not resist temptation, so we locked everything. Therefore, we had lots of locks and keys. Lots and lots!

Inside the house we had door keys, shelf keys, closet keys, dresser keys, desk keys, file drawer keys, pantry keys, and telephone keys, and – the list is endless. We also had a high fence around our house with a wide gate for cars and people, and that required a "key."

My realization of my personal frustration came when we moved into a two story house. At the end of the stairs, going into our bedroom area, there was a steel door which had to be locked. If robbers got into one part of the house, they still had to go through another locked door to get into the hall, and then the steel door was designed to prevent them from getting into the bedroom area. Now, that sounds great – good security! But, wait a minute! I am only 5'3" tall. If the keys were concealed above the door, I couldn't reach them. We couldn't hang them on a nail by the door – duh – and I couldn't always carry two extra keys.

One day we left the house, and Bill locked those two doors and said, "Honey, the keys are hidden just above the door."

We returned home and he went to his study, and I proceeded to the bedroom. I tiptoed and stretched, but could not reach the key. The steam started to emerge from the top of my head. Now, I tried to be patient (which unfortunately isn't one of my better points), but I felt like a child who was locked out of the house, and I launched my attack – against Bill!

"Honeyeeee," I yelled (trying to be kind), "don't lock these doors. I can't get in. What good is it to keep the thieves out, if I can't get into my own bedroom? I can't stand and wait for you to open the door for me."

My Key Frustration

Whew! My top had blown like a geyser, but I felt better after I released the pressure. Bill promised, under a chuckle, not to lock the door again.

One morning, I got up early and thought I would go out on the street and buy a newspaper – so I could get frustrated early! I went upstairs (where our kitchen and living room were). I looked at the two locks on the front door. I realized one of my keys was downstairs. Not being overly fond of exercise, I didn't want to mount the stairs again, or wake Bill up, so I went to the back door where the keys were available. I felt like an escaped prisoner as I walked out onto the driveway and toward the gate – only to realize I didn't have the gate key! TIK.

One day, during my frustration, I counted the keys we had to use. There were 35 keys – not including the car keys! I tell you the truth! Now, all of those were not major keys, but nevertheless, we had to use them. It's a job to just carry all of those keys. A man can manage to carry the important ones in his pockets, but a woman and her handbag are too often separated. Of course, my key chain could have been a pretty good weapon!

The problem was never solved, so I had to learn to live with my "key frustration" – KEYS! TIK.

Chapter 14

Worms in the Rice

Our food sources were limited. We had fresh fruit and vegetables – and we had to bargain over every kilo. I love bargaining, and accept it as a game – a challenge. But, I got tired of having to bargain over the price of every kilo of carrots, onions, potatoes, tomatoes, and everything fresh that we ate. We had little grocery stores – Uchumi's – where we could buy staples, cereal (two choices), some imported canned food, and milk. The milk was whole milk, and the cream was thick on top. When our kids came back to the States, they couldn't get used to using the milk without having to shake it.

Wyvonna and Shaleen came back to the States by themselves, and had to go to buy groceries. They wanted to buy cereal. When they saw a whole aisle of different cereal, they were overwhelmed! We had decent meat markets, but nothing like the States. Our meat was not wrapped in cellophane and stamped with a USDA government sticker.

Anything which was imported was expensive - $14.00 for a jar of mayonnaise! I made my own mayonnaise and mustard. I cooked from scratch! No quick, convenient foods in Kenya.

Some food, especially rice, would be unavailable at times. Of course, rice was a staple food for the Indians, and they would hoard it when it was in stock. We started hoarding also. Sometimes we would be out shopping, and we would see a lot of people queuing (standing in line). We knew they were waiting to buy something which was important, so we just jumped in line.

My friend, Cheryl, was living in Kitale where the supplies were even scarcer. They came into Nairobi about once a month to buy food. One time, she found the best grade of rice at an Indian shop in Kitale, so she stocked up. She bought about twenty-five kilos (more than fifty pounds) of rice. Shortly afterwards, they went on a short furlough. When they came back, she was horrified, and so disappointed, to find her rice full of bugs and worms. That rice was a rare commodity. She couldn't afford to throw it away. She quickly adapted to the situation, and continued to use it – carefully sifting the worms and bugs from it each time she cooked it! TIK. I have also sifted "things" from flour.

My Indian friends taught me how to preserve the large quantities of rice. Most people know you can keep rice by putting it in the freezer, but I didn't have a freezer, and neither did most of the Indians. They told me to get a large container – like a ten gallon plastic (or tin) container. The trick is to put a layer of rice, then a few drops of vegetable oil. Mix the rice with the oil so every grain is covered with oil. Continue layering it – rice and oil. Bugs and worms will never be a problem, and you can keep it indefinitely.

Kitale is in Western Kenya, and it is the last town before going into the bush country of Pokot and Turkana, where there were no stores for the missionaries in those areas. There wasn't a great supply of food even in Kitale, but when a truck would go from the bush into Kitale, the missionaries would send a list of things they would like if it was available. They were happy to get any kind of food supplies.

Cheryl said she bought a jar of Canadian peanut butter from an Indian duka (shop). When she got it home, she started to open it, and the foil seal had been loosened. She pulled it back, and saw the print of the finger which had swiped a good chunk out of it. She immediately returned it to the Indian. He put it back on the shelf.

She told me, "I am quite sure that peanut butter ended up in the supplies of some missionary in the bush who couldn't return it if she had wanted to. They ate it and were happy to get it – finger print and all!" TIK.

The merchant wasn't about to discard the peanut butter, because he knew he could pawn it off in the supplies going to the bush.

We love the Indian food, and occasionally I still have to go to an Indian restaurant for a good meal of curry and rice. We loved going to some of the little cafes and having samosas - little deep fried triangles of dough stuffed with meat and vegetables, and seasoned with various Indian spices. They are delicious with a squirt of lime juice on them.

We also loved the Kenyan "sacuma wiki." It means "pushing the week." The Kenyans try to grow the sacuma greens in their back yards, and when it's near the end of the week, and they don't have any more food, they eat the sacuma to finish the week. The greens in America which are closest to the sacuma greens are collards. I remove the bottom part of the stem, wash the leaves thoroughly, stack them, roll them up, and shred them from top to the bottom with a sharp knife. I sauté onions, and tomatoes, and a bit of cubed beef in hot oil, then add the greens with a little water and simmer them for about three hours. Instead of making chapattis as the Kenyans do, I serve the greens with warm tortillas. Delicious!

I never did acquire an appetite for "ugali" – the staple diet of the poor Kenyans. It is just finely ground white corn, mixed with hot water, formed into a round mold, and allowed to cool into a firm ball. They will not eat yellow corn, because they believe it will make them sterile!

One missionary was visiting in a rural village, and he was invited to eat lunch. He couldn't refuse in a polite way. He watched the women form the ugali with unwashed hands that had been doing various duties around the animals and children. A few men sat at the table with him as he ate. He tried to put the thoughts of the dirty hands out of his mind. It was also hard for him to eat the dead weevils that he found throughout the ugali. He didn't want to be offensive, so he prayed for grace and a strong stomach, and then ate them. After the meal was finished, he was surprised to see little weevils all around the edge of the plates of the Kenyans – they had not eaten them, but casually separated them from the ugali. TIK.

We lived in the city, and worked primarily with Indians, so we didn't have the opportunity to attend some of the rural African feasts where a goat was killed and cooked for dinner. The goat's head – eye balls included – was the delicacy which was given to the guests. I was never envious of this experience.

Chapter 15
Me? A Stock Car Driver?

Driving in Nairobi was another challenge. I didn't plan on ever driving there, but eventually the need to drive overpowered my fears. The Kenyans drove wherever their car would fit – either direction, on the sidewalk, or in the median. Everyone drove aggressively – or they would be run over! It was stressful at first, but after awhile it became a part of normal life in Kenya. There was no real road rage, but neither was there much respect for other drivers.

A policeman usually stood on every corner with a clipboard, but they didn't have a motorcycle or a car, so if a car didn't stop they couldn't give a ticket. They were only good for parking tickets. The Kenyans would pass on the median and then just squeeze back into traffic. It was wild.

One of our missionaries was driving in Nairobi with a pastor who was visiting from America. The missionary was trying to drive sensibly, but the other drivers would cut him off, pass on the wrong side, or almost run into him. He responded in the normal way – yelling at them, and driving the way they did.

The pastor finally said, "Brother, you don't have much compassion for these people, do you?"

The missionary responded, "You come over here and live for awhile, and we'll see how much compassion you have."

One day Shaleen and I went downtown, and I was looking for a parking place – which was hard to find. I saw an Indian get into his car, so I pulled up as close as I could to wait for him to back out. An African was coming from the other direction, and he also saw the car coming out. He pulled up close so he could whip into the space as soon as the Indian backed out. I started to tell him that I was waiting for the space, but he totally ignored me. Then I got annoyed – they didn't like me when I was angry! I pulled up closer and blocked the Indian, so he couldn't back out in my direction. He was patient, and waited while I withstood the African. Finally, I won the battle of words, and the African gave up, and drove away. I apologized to the Indian, and he just smiled. He understood! I learned how to drive agressively there. If you don't, you will be seriously hurt. TIK.

Entertaining Visitors

Bill was out of the country when a supporting pastor and his wife visited Kenya. They came to stay with me, and I took them downtown to shop, eat, and to sightsee. I had been driving there long enough by then that I could handle a car in most situations. I was driving at a reasonable speed and navigating through the traffic in our old Ford Cortina. There was something wrong with the car. Every time I applied the brakes, they made a startling screeching noise. I don't know what caused the noise, because we had new brakes. The car was just old. I was used to it, and didn't pay a lot of attention to the noise, but it sounded like I was about to hit something. The pastor was sitting in my passenger seat, and after awhile I started to notice that he would occasionally tense up in the traffic – and also when I had to use the brakes. It was nothing unusual for visitors to be a little uptight in the traffic, but he was getting nervous.

Finally, I said to him, "Am I scaring you?"

"Oh, no."

I almost laughed because I knew how he was feeling, but he was trying to be brave and macho.

When we got home after the first day, he said, "LaMoin, if you ever get tired of being a missionary, you can always come home, and get a job as a stockcar driver." I'm still not quite sure if that was a compliment or not!

The old Ford finally fell apart – literally! We were driving in it one day, and the whole right front a-frame collapsed. We couldn't buy parts for it in Kenya, so we contacted Eugene Worley, a missionary friend in England, and he sent us the parts to repair it. We had exhausted our efforts to get parts in Kenya, before we thought to contact Eugene. In the meantime, Bill made several calls to our supporting pastors in the States, and they donated enough money for us to buy another car. Bless their hearts! They were so good to help, and we thanked God for them. We repaired the car, and we were able to sell it to recoup some money from the repairs.

A Dead Body

If you accidently hit someone in Kenya, you didn't dare stop, because the mobs of people which quickly gathered would beat you to death. It sounds so unthinkable to the Western mind, but you have to play by their rules. TIK.

We were driving home one night in heavy traffic. The car in front of us tried to dodge something. He went on, and we saw the body of a man lying in the road in front of us. Bill was able to dodge it, but we didn't dare stop to try to offer assistance, or we could be accused of hitting him. I am sure he was already dead, because other cars weren't lucky enough to miss him. That scene stayed in my mind for a long time. I'm thankful we didn't have to feel the trauma of running over him.

You had to be brave and aggressive to drive there. It was also a bit dangerous to walk near the roads. The headline in the newspaper once read, "Minister of Parliament struck by a car while answering the call of nature."

In spite of all of the seriousness, some things were humorous. I read an article in the paper about a body which had been dragged from the river. It had been dismembered, stuffed in a burlap bag, and thrown in the river.

The police said, "We are treating this case as a homicide." Duh! TIK.

Don't Stop for the Baboons

In Kenya, you don't stop for dead bodies, and you don't stop for the baboons. We were driving to Mombasa when we came upon a pact of huge baboons. They appeared friendly, so Bill stopped the car to take some pictures. A big baboon suddenly jumped up on the car, and was trying to come into the window. Bill quickly rolled the window up, and thought the baboon would jump off the car when he started off. To our surprise, the baboon held on, and jumped on the hood by holding the windshield wiper – which he ripped off! They can be dangerous animals – especially when you don't feed them, and we were not supposed to feed them. Oh, well!

Chapter 16
The Nightmare on December 12

Our kids had recently come home from RVA for their Christmas holiday. Some of the other missionary kids and Simon and Carol were at our house one night. It was a nice night, and we decided to take a ride on the motorcycles. The kids were experienced riders, and we often rode together when they were home. They loved to ride, and it provided good family recreation. Before we left for the ride, we insisted that they wear good protection; helmets, boots, mufflers, and jackets.

Simon and Carol were on his bike, I was riding with Bill, Wyvonna was on Greg's bike, Shaleen was riding with Jay Piercey, and Russ Daniels was riding alone. We headed out toward the airport because there was a good divided road with a median, and it would also get us out of the city traffic. Simon was taking the lead. Bill and I were in the rear with all the kids in the middle so we could keep an eye on them. The traffic was not heavy, and we were enjoying the ride. We weren't sure who was right in front of us, because we had to pass a few cars along the way. Sometimes the kids would pass each other.

We were approaching a car. The bikes ahead had all successfully passed the car except the one directly in front of us. That bike went around, and was in the passing lane - side by side with the car to the left (we drove on the left side of the road). The road had no other cars on it. Suddenly, we saw headlights coming toward us – in the passing lane on our side of the road. It was a divided highway. The man was driving toward us on the wrong side. The bike ahead of us couldn't move to the left because of the car. There was no where for the driver to go. Then the oncoming car struck the bike.

My heart froze in my chest. I didn't even know who was on the bike in front of us, but I knew one of the kids had been hit. Bill quickly pulled onto the right shoulder of the road. I thought whoever it was would surely be dead. Sparks were flying from the bike as it skidded and bounced across the road in front of our headlight. I saw someone rolling down the road. Then I saw a big gold school letter on the jacket. It was Greg! *Oh, please, Lord, let them be alive.*

We jumped off the bike. Where was Wyvonna? The car we were passing had stopped. In front of the headlights of the car, I saw her lying on the other side of the road. As I was running, I saw Greg was getting up, so I knew he wasn't dead. I ran toward Wyvonna. (There is a big lump in my chest, and tears burn my eyes as I am writing this, and it has been many years ago.) It was such a nightmare, that the memories of that night still cause deep emotions.

Wyvonna was laying half on the road and half on the shoulder. She was conscious, but she was badly hurt. Greg was limping toward us with Bill's help. Shaleen had looked back and saw what happened, and had pounded on Jay's back to stop the bike. She was pulling her hair as she came running and screaming down the road. Of course, the other bikes stopped, and they all came to the scene.

I rushed to Wyvonna, and Bill helped Greg to get across the road where we were. Wyvonna's right leg had caught the impact of the car's bumper. It was crushed halfway between the knee and the ankle. Upon impact, her leg was jammed so hard that it also broke the femur halfway between her hip and knee.

The bone was sticking through her jeans, and her leg was rapidly swelling. It was already twice its normal size. Her leg was twisted up under her. I was trying to remove her helmet, and my hands were shaking. She removed it herself. She was calm even though she was in great pain. Maybe she was in shock.

We examined Greg. His hand on the bike had hit the car's windshield and broke it – and also three of his fingers. His neck had a cut. If it had not been for his thick muffler, the piece of glass would probably have killed him, but the muffler protected his throat. The impact of the car had knocked the heel off of his boot, and crushed his foot.

There were few ambulances, and we couldn't even call one. We were out of town – and no cell phones. Within minutes, while we were trying to quickly think what to do, a big white Mercedes came upon the scene. I know God sent those people that night. We couldn't call an ambulance, but God sent a chariot! An Indian couple was on their way to the airport to meet someone, but they stopped, and asked if they could help. (Okay, now the tears are coming as I remember that scene.)

"We've got to get these kids to the hospital." I said.

"Okay, we'll take you."

Bill and Simon had to carry Wyvonna to the car, but before they could pick her up, Bill gently straightened her leg.

"Oh, Dad, it hurts so much," she cried.

They put both the kids in the back seat of the car. Wyvonna's leg was stretched out across the seat. I got in front with the Indian couple. Bill had to stay behind at the scene until the police came. We got back into Nairobi and to the hospital in record time. Mr. Sharma was not concerned about any speed limits, neither were they concerned about who was arriving at the airport, nor the blood from the kids on their new car. They were wonderful!

When we arrived at the emergency room, Mr. Sharma ran inside, and asked for a stretcher. Instead, a nurse came with a wheelchair.

"We have accident victims here. We need a stretcher," he yelled.

"Oh, this will be okay," was the reply.

Mr. Sharma was irate. Greg could barely walk into the ER with our help. His foot was in bad shape. The attendant dragged Wyvonna out of the car, put her in the wheelchair, and took her inside. We were yelling at the nurse, and Wyvonna was holding her leg out straight with her own hands!

It was so chaotic when we entered the hospital. We were trying to get the best care for the kids while they were both groaning in pain. Mr. Sharma was giving orders to the staff. My emotions were barely holding together. I knew I had to be strong for the sake of the kids. I learned again that night that God's grace is sufficient – for any situation.

God started to talk to me when we entered the hospital. I felt Him so near, and He gave me peace. There have been a few times in my life that I have felt God's presence so near that I could almost physically touch Him. The night of the accident was one of those times. When I entered the emergency room, God walked in with me and talked to me! It was so real!

He said, *"All things work together for good to those who love God, (Romans 8:28). In everything give thanks: for this is the will of God in Christ Jesus for you, (I Thessalonians 5:18). Rejoice in the Lord always: and again I say, Rejoice, (Philippians 4:4). Trust in the Lord with all your heart, and lean not unto thine own understanding, (Proverbs 3:5, 6."*

Oh, yes, I know God was right there with us. I did not understand why the accident happened, and I certainly didn't feel like rejoicing, but I was able to relax, and to put it all in His hands.

Mr. Sharma said, "Don't let anyone treat them but Mr. Stewart. (A specialist is called "Mr." instead of "Dr.") He is an excellent British orthopedic surgeon. His reputation extends to England."

When we got inside the ER, he gave them orders to call Mr. Stewart. I am so glad he had that knowledge, because I didn't know about him.

They put the kids in treatment rooms which were partitioned with a curtain. Both of them were yelling in pain now. They were trying to be brave - and they were - but the pain was severe. They couldn't even get anything for pain until Mr. Stewart arrived at the hospital. The pain didn't keep Wyvonna from being upset when they had to cut off her new American jeans that had recently arrived from the States. The leg was three times its normal size, because the blood was collecting under the skin. Greg's jeans had large holes in the legs where he had rolled on the road.

Greg was yelling, and the nurse came in.

She came to his bed, and said, "Where do you hurt?" It was quite obvious his hand was mangled.

He held up his hand in her face and angrily asked, "Where do you think?"

While we waited for Mr. Stewart, Mr. Sharma stayed with Greg, and his wife sat with Wyvonna. I ran back and forth between them – trying to comfort both of them at the same time. I kept telling them the doctor would be there soon, and he would give them something to relieve the pain.

Mr. Stewart came, and after examining them, he put Wyvonna in traction. He said the bone had overlapped, and he could not operate until he could pull the bone back in alignment. He said he would have to do surgery on her the next day. She had lost over half of her blood, so they started giving her blood.

She was white as a sheet, but as new blood started into her body, color began to come back into her face. That was a few years before we knew about AIDS, and we had some fears later about what kind of blood she had gotten. But God spared her from getting infected blood.

The doctor said Greg had three broken, impacted fingers, and he would operate on him the next day also. Finally, the kids got some pain shots, which helped to relieve the pain. Greg's foot was not broken, but badly bruised. Mr. Stewart was going to put it in a cast, but later decided to just wrap it well.

Bill and the others had to remain at the accident scene until the police arrived, so the Sharmas stayed with me until they got to the hospital. I was so thankful to have these "angels" with me. They were so kind, gentle, and comforting. I have thanked God for them many times. Finally the kids were sedated and put into their rooms – on either end of the hospital. We ran between the rooms to be with both of them as much as possible.

Later, we discussed the accident. The man who hit the kids was drunk, and he was driving on the wrong side of the road - without his lights. When he saw the bike in front of him, he quickly turned on the lights, and when Greg saw the lights, he swerved to the left as much as he could without hitting the car that he was passing. If he had not swerved, he and Wyvonna would not be with us today. It was enough to keep from being hit head on. The man tried to drive his luxury car away, but when he hit the bike, it burst his front tire. He and his passengers got out of the car, and ran across a field and got away.

Bill and the others witnessed another wreck before the police showed up. While they were waiting for the police, another car came. They tried to wave him down before he got to the scene. Unlike in America, the bike had to be left in the road for police inspection. He tried to miss the bike, but he hit it, lost control of his car, went up on two wheels, and overturned. It totaled his car, but he walked away unhurt. He was the policeman in charge of the traffic division! He was also drunk.

We left the hospital at three o'clock in the morning, after the kids went to sleep. We had to be back early the next morning for Wyvonna's surgery. It was useless to try to sleep when we did get home. Every time I closed my eyes, I saw the whole scene again; the car lights in front of us, sparks flying from the bike, Greg rolling down the road, and Wyvonna at the side of the road. I thought I would never close my eyes again without seeing that scene – and it took a long time.

The next day some of our missionary friends came to sit with us during the surgeries. Wyvonna went to surgery first. After about three hours, I became frightened. *Did they run into complications? Have they had to amputate her leg? Does part of the bone have to be removed?* My imagination was going wild – until God spoke, *"Be not afraid."*

After about six hours, Mr. Stewart came out and told us everything was fine, and she was out of danger. Then Greg went in for surgery. Again we waited for about three hours. Dr. Stewart put pins in his fingers to hold the bones, but after three days, Greg had to go back into surgery for the doctor to try to repair his fingers.

I am so eternally grateful for Mr. Stewart. He flunked on bedside manners, but with God guiding his hands, he performed a miracle on Wyvonna. He said her leg was crushed, and he had to put the pieces back together like a puzzle. Praise God, he didn't remove any of the bone. He put two stainless steel plates in the leg to hold the bones together – one above the knee and one below the knee. Each of them was one foot long, and about an inch wide. He attached the plates to the bone with screws about three quarters of an inch long.

Mr. Stewart said Greg would have more permanent damage from his broken fingers than Wyvonna would have on her leg. The doctor did the best he could, but Greg's ring and pinky fingers were permanently bent. The joints were too badly damaged for the fingers to heal straight.

We still had to pray that no infection would develop in the bones in Wyvonna's leg. One Indian friend didn't consider the impact of his words, when he told us about one of his relatives who had a similar operation. Later infection developed in the bone, and part of the bone had to be removed, which left the person with a bad limp. I didn't need that information.

Mr. Stewart was not a Christian, but he said, "Somebody up there was watching over her. She doesn't even have any nerve damage." Since that time, I have had many nightmares from thinking about what damage could have been done to her. Can you imagine? Spinal damage, nerve damage – she could have been paralyzed! We didn't have anything to make a splint with. We just had to do the best we could to get her to a doctor. Our thoughts were to save her life. Again, our angel was at the scene.

Greg came home from the hospital in a week, walking with crutches, with a soft cast on his foot and ankle, splints on his fingers, and pins in the bones. But, Wyvonna was in the hospital for three weeks. She opened her Christmas gifts while her leg was suspended in the air in a traction device. She lost twenty pounds in those three weeks. Mr. Stewart said she would have to learn to walk again - that frightened me.

My strong willed daughter said, "That is not going to happen. I learned to walk once, and I will not learn to walk again. I will show him I can walk when I get out of this bed."

She was so weak the first time they got her out of bed – after almost three weeks – she almost fainted. She had to walk with crutches when she left the hospital, but she didn't have to learn to walk again.

Wyvonna had a large open wound where the bumper had hit her leg and crushed it. She has been blessed with a strong will, and a huge tolerance for pain. She watched while the nurses treated it and changed the bandages. I couldn't bear to look at it, neither could some of her school friends who came to visit her.

"Let me see it," a friend asked.

"Are you sure you want to look at it? It looks pretty bad." Wyvonna said.

"Yes, I'll be fine."

Wyvonna pulled the bandage back so she could see – and her friend promptly fainted!

When Mary, our house girl, heard about the accident, she almost went hysterical. She loved the kids and she was upset. She wanted to go to the hospital to visit Wyvonna.

I said, "Now, Mary, when you see her, don't cry, because it will make her feel worse."

"Oh, missus, I won't cry."

Just before we got to the room, I told her again. We walked into the room, and Mary ran over, and hugged Wyvonna. Then she put her head on the bed and just sobbed.

Wyvonna said, "Its okay, Mary. Don't cry. I'm going to be fine."

Many people commented about how strong Wyvonna was throughout the terrible ordeal.

I'm so thankful to God, and so happy to tell you that today, even though she has bad scars, she has no limp. She has a slight concave in her leg where the open wound was, but she is fine. She could easily have lost her leg, or been paralyzed - or they both could have been killed. God is so good.

What happened to the driver?

The police located the driver – he left his car behind. He was employed by a prestigious law firm in Nairobi. He was

The Nightmare on December 12

charged with reckless driving, drunken driving, driving on the wrong side of the road, grievous bodily harm, and leaving the scene of the accident.

I was irate as we sat in the courtroom with our two injured children. He sat with a smirk on his ugly face; with full confidence this whole thing was just a waste of his time.

A female judge heard the charges. We had witnesses there – including the Indian man who was driving the car that Greg was passing. But, the judge never gave them a chance to speak.

In the end, the guy who hit them was fined the equivalent of $50.00 and released. They didn't even suspend his license. He smiled and left the courtroom.

I can't remember when I have been angrier than I was then. It was quite evident he knew the judge and had bribed her. In Kenya, it is customary to bow to the judge when he/she enters the courtroom, and when you leave the room. She was still on the bench when we left. I glared at her, and I walked erectly out. I wasn't about to bow to her!

We sued the insurance company for damages. They finally paid for the totaled motorcycle, all the medical bills, and compensated Wyvonna with $11,000.00 and $3,000 for Greg. It certainly wasn't much compensation for the pain and suffering, and the permanent damage they suffered, but – TIK.

Greg was able to go back to school when the vacation was over, but Wyvonna had to stay at home for a few weeks longer. We got homework for her to do, so she didn't get behind. She later went back to school on crutches. It was extremely difficult for her.

I was amazed at the grace God gave to me after it was all over. God even removed the hate which I had for the man who hit them. Truly by the grace of my heavenly Father, I felt a burden for his soul. I came to the place where I wrote him a long letter. I told him I had hated him for what he did to my children, but God had placed forgiveness in my heart for him.

I explained to him that the Bible teaches that we are all sinners – born into sin because of the sin of Adam and Eve. I told him that Jesus said we would go to Hell if we are not born again. I wrote that Jesus Christ died for his sin as well as for mine. But he had to humble himself, and believe Jesus Christ was the only way to heaven (John 14:6). I told him he would have to believe Jesus died, was buried, and rose again, and if he would ask Jesus to forgive him for all of his sin, he would be saved, and go to heaven when he died. I mailed the letter to him – but I never heard from him. God promised His word would not return void. So, if that man dies without Christ, my hands are clean of any of his blood.

I am so thankful God removed the bitterness from my heart. It was definitely the grace of God, because otherwise, I could not have forgiven him.

God's Grace is Sufficient

During the fifty years we have been missionaries, there have been many tests and trials. Sometimes the warfare with Satan has been so difficult. If it had not been for God's grace, we would have been defeated and put out of the ministry. However, even though the pressures have sometimes been almost humanly impossible to bear – His grace has always proven sufficient.

God's grace was again put to the test that night of December 12. Satan knows the love for my children is my weakest point. If he hurts them, he hurts me. He thought he could use this accident to break my emotions. I had suffered an emotional breakdown seven years prior in Australia. I am sure he planned to kill two of our children, and cause me to have another breakdown to destroy my husband's ministry. But, praise God – His grace is sufficient. God had healed me from the breakdown, and he proved it. If I was going to have one, it would have been that night. When I look back on those first few days after their accident, I am amazed how God gave me peace that passes my understanding.

When Bill and I saw the car hit our children, I thought they were dead, but God calmed me. When I was sitting on the side of the road with my hands under the heads of my children, I had peace. Of course, I felt the horrible chills of fear race through my body as any mother would feel. I could have gone completely hysterical when I looked at my son's broken hand, crushed foot, and bleeding neck. It was not easy to look at my daughter's leg which was swollen to twice its normal size, with the bone in the thigh sticking out through her jeans, and the lower part of her leg broken, crushed, and twisted under her. But, God calmed me. When I think back to that night, I realize how God watched over them in directing Mr. and Mrs. Sharma to the scene. God was there when we put her in the car without a splint.

Bill was preaching in the church service the Sunday after the accident, and my mind was wandering. I flipped open my Bible, and my eyes went immediately to (Ephesians 3:13), "Wherefore I desire that ye faint not at my tribulations for you, which is your glory." I was stunned. I knew God had spoken to me, but I didn't understand all of it. I understood when He told me to not faint at the tribulations. I was comforted by the scripture. But glory? *Lord, I don't want any glory. Glory belongs to you only.* I must admit I still don't understand that part of the verse. I just hung on to the part about fainting not at the tribulations. It was a comfort to me even if I didn't understand it – God spoke to me.

One of my friends asked me, "Don't you just wonder why God let this happen?"

I said, "No, I will never ask God 'why' because He has permitted them to survive. He has been with me, and comforted me. He told me to thank Him for everything, so I thank Him for their lives, and I will not ask 'why'."

Our angels were camped around about us that night.

Wyvonna said, "I felt like someone lifted me from the bike, carried me across the road, and gently laid me down." (Psalm 91:11-12) says, "He shall give his angels charge over thee, to keep thee in all thy ways. They shall bear thee up in their hands lest thou dash they foot against a stone."

They had no facial or head injuries. Their helmets were not cracked, or broken. Praise be to God only.

The kids went back to RVA to finish the school year. Wyvonna went on crutches and Greg still wore splints and a cast. They were great through the whole terrible ordeal of the accident, and then didn't complain when it was time to go back to school.

Chapter 17
The Shooting Started at Midnight

In July, the year after the accident, we went to RVA to attend Wyvonna's and Shaleen's graduation from high school. Graduation in America is always a happy time, but for the RVA graduates, it was bitter sweet. They were happy to be graduating, but they knew it meant they would probably never see their friends again on this earth. These kids were from all parts of the world. They had friends from Israel, Norway, and other countries besides the United States. Also, it meant the kids would be leaving Kenya – and their families – to return to the United States to go to college. So, there were many mixed emotions – with the graduates and the families.

There were many tears that day as the graduates tossed their caps in the air, and then hugged goodbye as they each loaded their material belongings into the family cars to separate to the ends of the earth, and to embark upon a whole new life alone.

Our daughters were planning to leave in a couple of weeks to return to the States to enter college. We, as parents, had no idea what emotions were running wild in their hearts. Oh, we knew they would dread the parting from us, but we didn't know they were not returning "home." My and Bill's roots are in America, but not so with our children.

However, in our minds they were going home. They should be excited. No, they were not excited, because to them, they would be going to virtually a foreign country by themselves. They would have to endure the culture shock of America without us. No one can fully understand except another missionary kid.

They had already been accepted into the college, and we had their plane tickets in hand. I was going to fly home with them to get them settled. They were packing the day before we were to leave. They were doing so much arguing, and finally I became concerned. It was quite evident they were having some problems.

I said to them, "You don't want to leave, do you?" They tried to avoid telling me the truth, but I knew this was what was causing their short tempers. I told Bill we needed to talk. He called them into our room, and we all lay down together on our bed. They finally confessed they didn't want to leave.

Bill said, "Then you don't have to leave."

"But we have no choice. You already have the plane tickets."

"The tickets can be cancelled. You're not going anywhere."

They were worried about the money for the tickets, but we convinced them we could get a refund. Then the happiness returned. They stayed on with us for six months before they became bored and decided it was time for them to leave.

Forced to Move

Mary, her husband, and their children lived in the workers quarters in the back of our triplex. The servants for the landlord and the neighbors also lived there. Everyone lived peacefully, and got along well together.

One night Mary and her husband had a big fight. During the fight, Mary almost bit his thumb off. It was bad, and he had to have medical treatment. He had been drinking, and when he started a fight, she finished it. She wouldn't let him push her around. We were not aware of anything going on, but the next day, the servants reported it to the landlord.

We had become quite fond of our town house, but we were given a choice by the landlord – get rid of Mary or move! This was totally unexpected and unwanted. We loved Mary too much to get rid of her, so we choose to find another place to live.

It was difficult to find another house which we could afford, but we finally heard of an old house across town that a missionary was vacating, so we rented it. It wasn't as nice as our town house, but we had exhausted our efforts to find anything else. It was a single house with three bedrooms, bath, kitchen, and a combined dining and living room. It also had servants' quarters in the back, and a big yard. Mary was happy because they would not have other servants living so close to them. We had a long talk with her and her husband, and laid down the law to them – there would be no fighting! Tobias agreed to not drink - which had caused the problems. He was a nice guy otherwise.

Moving is always difficult, but there were always more problems in Kenya. It was a hassle to get the utilities turned on and to get a telephone. Everything exhausted the patience. Some of the Indians helped us, and we finally completed our move on Saturday.

We were dead tired, but our three children wanted to go with some of their friends to a movie in Nairobi. They usually went to a movie, and then went to the popular Thorn Tree sidewalk restaurant after the movie. They came home about 11 o'clock, and we all went to bed.

The Coup of August 1, 1982

We were sound asleep when I was awakened by a knocking on our bedroom window at 6 o'clock in the morning. I heard Mary calling me.

"Missus, wake up. We have big problems with the government."

Half asleep, I made my way to the window, opened it, and asked, "What problems, Mary? What have we done?" I thought, during the move, we had broken some Kenyan law through ignorance.

"Oh, you haven't done anything. I think they have killed President Moi."

Well, I was suddenly fully awake! "Bill, did you hear that?"

"Yes."

"Mary, come around to the door, and I'll let you in."

She came in, and quickly told us all she knew. She had heard an early radio report that the Kenyan Air Force had staged a coup to over throw the government. Tobias worked in a government office in the city, and he had not come home that night. She was afraid he might be dead.

We turned on the television and heard, "Kenya is now in the hands of the People's Redemption Council. We are warning everyone to stay inside your homes, and you will not be hurt. Again, stay inside your homes. Do not go outside. Stay off the streets. The radio and television stations are now controlled by the People's Redemption Council." That was *very* bad! While we were listening to the television, Tobias finally made his way home safely, and he reported that people were being killed all over Nairobi.

We didn't know if they had killed President Moi. We could hear the shooting. It was close. We listened. Round after round of automatic gunfire!

Bill and I quickly began to think what we would have to take with us in case of evacuation – if evacuation was even possible. We knew we would have to leave most everything behind except the clothes on our backs. We would take important papers and passports. *How long did we have? How would we be notified of evacuation? Could we make it through the gunfire to the pickup point?* Many, many questions raced through our minds. But, we tried to stay calm for the sake of our children.

The kids were still sleeping, but when they heard us talking to Mary, they got up and came into the living room.

"What's going on?" they asked.

We tried to cover the truth for fear they would be upset, but they knew something was terribly wrong. Finally, we had to tell them the truth. They gave each other a knowing look. Then they told us that when they were leaving the night before to return home, they had heard the gunfire. They thought it was fireworks. God had protected our children.

We watched the television for any news, while we listened to the increasing gunfire outside. Soon, Simon came to the house. He had risked his life to come to check on us.

"It's bad out there, but I had to come to check on you. Don't leave the house. The Kenya Air Force attacked the radio and television stations, and captured them - with heavy casualties. They also commandeered the airport, and other strategic installations. On the way, I saw an ambulance going to pick up some injured men. Soldiers stopped it and asked where they were going. Then they shot the driver, pulled him out of the ambulance and commandeered the vehicle. They are just shooting wide. They shoot at anything that moves."

We stayed inside the house for three days, and listened to the sporadic gunfire. Finally, everything calmed down. We learned that President Moi was still alive, and he had ordered the Army to suppress the Air Force. The Army went on another killing spree, but the coup was finally controlled, and President Moi was back in power.

Nairobi was in ruins. The stores were all looted and literally cleaned out. Maasai broke into butcher shops and stole meat

– the most valuable thing to them. Others went for precious stones, jewelry, clothing, groceries, and electronics. Slum dwellers looted television sets only to be stranded with them since they had no electricity. TIK.

One man with a gun, (member of the Army or Air Force) went to the Hilton – intent on having sex with a white woman. He raped a tourist on the stairs, but died on his way out in a hail of bullets.

Raping, plundering, and killings went on in many parts of Nairobi. We learned later that gangs of men had come within two blocks of our house; raping and looting houses of everything they could carry out. Again, God protected us.

Several hundred people were killed – contrary to the news reports. People had to step over numerous bodies on the streets. Later, the bodies were piled on top of each other in the morgue while they waited for family members to identify them. The stench permeated the area.

A dawn to dusk curfew was placed upon the city for at least a month. After three days, we finally felt that we could leave the house. We drove down the still quiet streets into the city. It made us nervous to see young, trigger-happy soldiers everywhere on the streets. Once we were stopped at gunpoint, and the car was searched. That was not a good feeling.

All over the city we saw cars with bullet holes in them. When we arrived downtown, we could hardly believe our eyes. The paper and litter in all the streets were knee high. Every store had been ransacked. The iron bars which covered the doors and windows had been pulled away with trucks in order to gain entrance. The boxes and papers from the loot had been dropped in the streets. It was truly a war zone.

The university students are usually always involved in political unrest in a third world country, and it was true in this attempted coup. A bus load of students from the university had been the target of the Army as they passed our former house. The soldiers opened fire on them and killed most of them in front of the townhouse from where we had just moved. There were bullet holes in the house. The coup was not a surprise to our Lord, and he had permitted the fight between Mary and her husband in order to protect us. We had moved just hours before it began.

President Moi exercised strict vengeance. He immediately ordered several people to be executed – including Senior Private Hezekiah Ochuka, who had master-mined the coup. He controlled Kenya for a period of thirty minutes - and died for it.

"The angel of the Lord campeth round about them that fear him, and delivereth them." (Psalm 34:7). I am so comforted to know we do have guardian angels. Ours have been tested many times and proven to be real. What a blessing! The song, "Sheltered in the Arms of God" has always been a blessing to me. If we are in His arms – what can harm us? He is with us in the storm, and will protect us until it passes by.

Soon after the coup, Mary took a vacation and went out of town to see her relatives. She rode on a bus. We had given her some blankets and other things. She was taking some of it with her. We heard the police were searching all the buses, and taking things from passengers which they thought had been stolen in the coup. They were attempting to return things to their rightful owners. Of course, the police were also abusing the people in taking things they knew had not been stolen. TIK.

I said, "Mary, maybe you should leave those things home. The police might take them away from you."

"If they try to take my things, I will kill somebody." She got through safely.

Chapter 18
Greg Almost Died

After the coup, Greg went back to RVA – alone this time. Wyvonna and Shaleen were with us in Nairobi. Greg had adjusted well to RVA and had many friends, so he didn't mind going back. But, it was hard for me to leave him there by himself. Each time we visited him that year, my heart would crack a little more as we left him standing alone in front of his dorm. We would wave to each other until we drove out of sight, and then I would cry half way back to Nairobi. One more year and he would graduate and return to the States. If you ask me what I consider as the hardest part of missionary work, I would not hesitate to say, "Separation from my children."

I decided to take a short trip back to the States to see my aging parents. The girls were home to stay with Bill, and Mary would take good care of all of them.

I took the Pan Am "Red Eye." The flight was about 22 hours to New York. Even though I am a bit claustrophobic, I have never had a problem flying. However, after such a long time being restricted in a window seat with no leg room, panic almost overtook me about an hour away from landing in New York. I thought, *if I don't get out of this seat, I am going to start screaming.* I had to disturb the passenger who was sitting next to me by asking to get out. I thought I *had* to get into the aisle, or they would see some *major* disturbance. After I was able to stretch, and to walk up and down the aisle, I felt much better.

I enjoyed being with my family, and just not having any responsibilities for awhile. I even went to Houston to visit with some old friends, Carl and Lora Beth Wright. Carl let me use his car, and I drove to Galveston to visit with my brother and his family. When I returned to Houston, Carl and Lora Beth asked me if I'd had any trouble with directions or driving through Houston.

"Oh, no. It was such a pleasure to drive where everyone obeys the rules of the road, and stays in their own lane. It was so sane and wonderful!" I gushed.

They looked at each other in shock, and said, "If she thinks the Houston traffic is easy, we'd better call the newspaper, and tell them. This will make quite a story."

I was back at my parent's house when I received a phone call from Bill in Kenya.

"I need to tell you that Greg is sick."

I panicked, "What's wrong with him? What happened?"

"Well, he came home for the weekend, and didn't feel well. His face was puffy and he had what appeared to be an infected pimple on his chin. He was putting on weight abnormally fast. I took him to the doctor, and during the examination, the doctor realized his kidneys were not functioning normally. He admitted him immediately to the hospital for observation. Not long afterwards, Greg started having convulsions. His head would draw to the side, and he had no control over his body."

"The doctor diagnosed the condition as 'acute glomerulonephritis.' It is an acute infection of the kidneys. The doctor feels it is a result of a bacterial infection from the pimple. He is in the hospital, and is being treated. I will let you know as soon as I know anything new."

When I hung up, I grabbed my mother's doctor book, and looked up the disease. I was terrified when I learned his condition could cause death! I felt so helpless. Here I was 10,000 miles away, and my son was so sick. I felt like a terrible mother, because I was not with him.

"I should not have left Kenya," I told my mother.

"You didn't know this was going to happen, so don't blame yourself."

There was no way I could get to him quickly. It would take at least three or four days to arrange a flight and make the trip. I agonized with guilt. A son needs his mother when he's sick. I finally gained control of my emotions, and started praying for God to heal him. I should have done that before I panicked, but I am a mother, and there was a wide ocean between my son and me. But God is not restricted by land and sea. His eyes were on my son, and I had instant contact with Him. He could do, in my absence, what I could not do if I was holding Greg's hand in mine. I poured out my fears to God, and begged him to heal my son.

The next day, Bill called back. Greg was much better, and the convulsions had stopped. He had good medical care, and was past the worse of the illness. He would be okay.

I still felt guilty that I could not be there with him. Although, I was thankful to know my heavenly father had given wisdom and knowledge to his medical staff, and God had answered my prayers. I immediately made arrangements to return to Kenya.

Have you ever noticed that many times we can remember things to laugh about after a terrifying experience? Greg was scared when he was in the hospital, because he didn't know how serious his condition might be. One night he overheard his doctor talking to someone in the hall just outside his room. He was discussing a kidney transplant. The next morning the doctor came in to see Greg.

Greg said, "I want to know the truth. How bad is my condition?"

"Oh, you're going to be okay."

"Well, I heard you talking about doing a kidney transplant."

"Oh, I wasn't talking about you. There are six other kidney patients in other rooms."

Greg got angry, "Then why are you standing out in the hall discussing a kidney transplant when we can all hear you?"

I think it was a reasonable rebuke.

Our Daughters Returned to America

After being with us for six months after their graduation, Wyvonna and Shaleen decided they wanted to return to America and enroll in Baptist Bible College – our alma mater. There was nothing for them to do in Kenya. They couldn't work there, nor further their education. Social contacts and activity was limited, so they needed to get on with their lives. They were accepted by BBC, and made plans to leave after Christmas.

We didn't know how we were going to get all of their worldly possessions out of Kenya with them. Each person was allowed only forty-four pounds of luggage on the flight. I have never been one to quickly accept defeat, so Bill and I went to the office of the airlines. We talked to the manager, and explained to him that the girls had been living in Kenya, and now they were moving back to America. They needed to take all of their things with them, but we couldn't afford to pay the high cost of shipping. We prayed a lot, and we appealed to his better nature. He finally gave us a written letter to give to the officials at the airport to wave all over-weight luggage for them!

We took them to the airport with stuffed suitcases, foot lockers, and flight bags! When we presented the letter at check-in, they tagged the entire mound of luggage and waved it through. That was a miracle of God, because we always approached the airport – going or coming – with great fear and apprehension.

God gave sufficient grace to say goodbye to our precious daughters. I would miss them, but I also knew the parting was best for them. A friend from RVA – another missionary daughter – traveled with them, so I prayed they would enjoy the trip. God gave me wonderful peace that they would be okay.

Chapter 19
More Surgery for Wyvonna

Wyvonna and Shaleen had a good trip back to the States. Our missionary friends, Jerry and Shari Piercey were home on furlough and met them at the airport. They stayed with the Pierceys until they moved into the college dorm. The adjustment was not easy, but they bravely handled it.

They had been in the States about two months when we received a phone call from Shari. She told us the plate on the femur in Wyvonna's leg had broken, and she would have to have surgery. I am not sure what happened, but she had fallen in the shower at RVA before she graduated. Maybe the fall cracked the steel plate – it didn't seem possible, but…. TIK.

She had seen an excellent orthopedic surgeon in Springfield who was a member of the church she was attending. He said the plate was broken, and the bone was growing crooked - and her leg was bowing. It was quite visible. He would have to remove the plate, and replace it with a new one. This happened about a year after her surgery in Nairobi.

I flew home for the surgery which lasted nine hours. I am thankful that Shari sat with me during the long surgery. I knew Wyvonna had a good doctor, but it was agonizing to wonder what was going on behind those closed doors.

Dr. Holland removed the plate, took bone from her hip, grafted it into the femur, and put in a new plate. He did the bone graft because he was afraid it might not heal since it was an old wound. The bone below her knee had healed, so he removed that plate. A plastic surgeon then did some repair work on her lower leg to eliminate a lot of the scaring. The poor kid was cut from her hip to her ankle, and then came out of the hospital in a full leg cast for four months.

I stayed with the girls for a month, but I couldn't remain in the States. Greg was graduating from school soon. I couldn't miss his graduation, and Bill needed me. I was torn between my responsibilities for the ones who were so firmly attached to my heart.

Wyvonna couldn't go back to school in her leg cast. Many of her classes were upstairs, and she couldn't climb stairs. Shaleen wasn't too happy in school at the time, so she dropped out, and I got an apartment for them. They had a good neighbor who would watch over them. Shaleen got a job, and our good pastor friend, Billy Barrs, bought a car for them.

I got them settled into the apartment, stayed on for a couple of weeks, and prayed God would comfort them - and me - as I boarded a plane for Kenya. They would have to live alone for almost four months until we returned for furlough.

Those were hard times for all of us, but God's grace is sufficient, and we survived. It was far harder on the girls, because they had to have a crash course in doing a lot of things on their own which were unfamiliar to them. They missed us terribly, and even though we were helping financially, they were short on money. They never let us know, but sometimes, they had only flour in the house to eat, so they made African chapattis with flour and water.

It breaks my heart even now when I think of the hardships they endured because we were missionaries. Sometimes I throw a pity party, and I remind God of all I have sacrificed to serve Him. Oh, don't judge me – I'll bet you have done the same thing. One day, I told Him I just didn't understand why some things have turned out contrary to my liking. *I have served you faithfully all these years, and we've left our country and family. My kids have suffered. I have done everything I could to please you, blah, blah, blah!* Immediately after I finished my complaining, God spoke!

He said, "*That is only your reasonable service,* (Romans 12:1)."

Ouch! That hurt. But He wasn't finished with me.

He went on to say, "*Ye have not yet resisted unto blood, striving against sin,* (Hebrews 12:4)." Oh, that stung even more. I felt so guilty!

God, I'm sorry. Please forgive me.

I have hurt so much, and many times I felt that a vice was on my heart. But, then I think of all of the Christians – even the thousands since World War II – who have been imprisoned in Communist countries for their faith in Christ. And many are in prison now. They have endured such horrible things which our minds have a hard time to understand. And I think I've had it rough! Compared to those in the wretched Communist prisons, I have had a life of luxury tiptoeing through the tulips in the land of sugar canes and lollipops. And so have you! We really don't know what suffering is. If you are unconvinced, read the book, "In God's Underground" by Richard Wurmbrand.

Chapter 20
A Much Needed Furlough

It was July 1983, and time for Greg to graduate from RVA. He had been accepted into Liberty Baptist University. It was also time for us to take a furlough.

We packed everything we had, and put it into storage. Simon and Carol rented the house we vacated, and he was assuming leadership of the church in our absence.

After moving out of the house, we had about two weeks to wait until Greg's graduation. We moved our suitcases into another missionary's home to house-sit for them while they were gone. It was a small two-story townhouse with narrow concrete steps going up to the second floor.

One morning I left Bill to sleep. I gathered the dirty clothes, and put them in a big Kenyan laundry basket. I silently crept out of the bedroom to get an early start on washing the clothes. The basket was large and heavy. I was trying to look around it as I started down the steps. You guessed it – I missed a step. I tumbled down the flight of steps to the small landing, and then down the remaining five steps onto the concrete floor below. The basket rolled down with me, and landed on top of me. Clothes were strewn over me and the floor. I couldn't get up. It did not create a positive attitude within me! Neither was I praising the Lord! I would have seriously hurt someone if they told me that I would get my rewards in Heaven. I just lay there trying to determine if I was badly hurt. My legs were really hurting, but I didn't think I had any broken bones.

Then I heard a voice from above – no, it wasn't God!

Bill called, "Are you okay?"

Now, it wasn't his fault, so why did I feel angry at him? Well, he could have made the effort to come to check on me. After all, this happened while I was trying to be a good wife, and wash his dirty clothes! I was in pain, and I was just angry! And he happened to be in the same house.

"Oh, I am half dead down here while you are sleeping." I had to take out my frustration on someone, didn't I?

He came down and helped me to get up. I hurt, but I picked up the clothes, and went outside to do the laundry. I had to fill the wringer washing machine by hand. It sure would have been easier to dump them into an automatic washer. TIK.

My legs were still hurting when we went up the mountain to attend Greg's graduation. That brought another round of mixed emotions. I was happy to see Greg graduate, but I knew that soon I would have to endure another long separation. Would it never end? No, life goes on, and separation and heartache are a part of life.

The day after Greg graduated, we headed to the airport. We had managed, again, to get the airlines to wave his overweight luggage. It was a relief to be free from worry about having to pay a large amount of money. Airports have always created stress for me. I am so thankful that when I take my last trip – to Heaven – I will not have to pack or worry about paying for overweight luggage. I won't even have to go through those tiring security checks!

My legs ached and swelled so much on the flight. They were still hurting from my tumbling down the stairs. I never went to the doctor. When I look back on that incident, I am surprised that I didn't die from blood clots. But, God wasn't finished with me yet. I still had many more miles to travel and many more storms to go through.

Rome

We had missionaries in Rome, Italy, and they were gracious enough to invite us to stay with them so we could do some sightseeing. (Shaleen has never forgiven us for taking Greg through Italy and not her.)

Lee spoke Italian fluently – without even an accent – and acted as our tour guide in Rome. It was unfortunate that we happened to be there when all of Europe was experiencing an unusual heat wave, but that didn't stop us.

Lee showed us a lot of the major tourist sites; the Colosseum, St. Peter's Basilica, the Vatican City, the Fountain of Trevi, the Spanish Steps, and many others. We walked all over Rome in scorching heat. I think it fried my brain, because I can't even remember all the places we saw.

His wife went with us on a day trip by plane to Venice. One day there was not enough, but we saw San Marco's square with the million pigeons. We toured St. Mark's Basilica, and walked across Rialto Bridge. I was fascinated by the Grand Canal with all the traffic on the water. Water taxis, gondolas, ambulances, police boats – everything goes on water instead of on pavement. I would love to return to Venice someday and explore the city leisurely. I wanted a ride in the famous gondolas, but they were too expensive for our budget. Maybe before I die, I will return to Venice.

Another day, we took a train south to Naples, and then to Sorrento. We had to change trains in Naples, so we had lunch there in the train station restaurant. The waiter got mad at me, because I didn't want to order the special. I requested a menu

– politely. He was angry. I guess he didn't want to do the little extra work. The Italians are very volatile. We finally got some food, and then we walked around Naples for awhile, until it was time to take the train on to Sorrento.

Sorrento is a small town located over white steep cliffs, and offers a fantastic view over the Bay of Naples. It was so beautiful! I wish I could have been there for a week, but it was just a day trip, and we packed a lot into those hours. We went to a big open air market where leather was a major attraction. The skilled Italian workers made such beautiful clothing from the fine glove leather. Bill and Greg bought leather jackets for just a few dollars.

We walked around the town, and looked at all of the fine Italian works of art. I was amazed when we watched a wood worker making serving trays, tea carts, and all sorts of souvenirs of inlaid wood. He took several layers of thin wood, stacked them, put them under a small saw blade, and cut out little flowers or whatever design he was making. Then he would arrange them to form a beautiful pattern for what he was making. After he had them arranged in the wood the way he wanted them, he would then paint them, and finish by putting several coats of shellac or polyurethane on top. He made pictures and all kinds of things.

I purchased a large serving tray and a tea cart. The tea cart had to be assembled later, but he wrapped them, and shipped them home for us. I was so disappointed when the tea cart arrived. It had been handled roughly in shipping, and one corner was cracked. TIK? However, I used it for many years until it had to be retired.

I loved Sorrento, and was not ready to board the train to take us back to Rome. We stayed for a week in Italy, and enjoyed it so much. We were so thankful to Lee and his family for their gracious hospitality.

Chapter 21
A Maniac Mechanic

It was wonderful to be met at the airport by our two beautiful daughters. It had been less than four months, but seemed much longer. Wyvonna was not wearing the leg cast. It had been removed a few weeks before, and her leg had healed beautifully.

We went directly to their apartment to stay until we had to take Greg to Liberty. I was shocked when I opened their refrigerator. There was no food! I almost cried when I found out how they had been skimping to made ends meet.

"Why didn't you tell us you had no food?" I cried.

"We didn't want to trouble you. We felt we had to make it on our own."

"Come on. We're going to the store." We went to a big supermarket, and I started to load up that grocery basket.

"Are you sure we can get all of this stuff?" they asked.

"Whatever you want, throw it in. You're not going to starve any more."

We loaded the basket full. Later, they said they couldn't believe we could actually buy all of that food. They had been getting by on so little, so they were amazed by all the food I bought. Bless their hearts. It still makes me so sad I could cry while I am writing this. We thought they were doing fine with

Shaleen working, and with us paying for Wyvonna's half of the bills. I guess I had not figured the hidden costs.

The time came too soon for us to take Greg to Lynchburg, Virginia. He was starting his freshman year at Liberty Baptist University. Another piece of my heart died when we had to drive away and leave him there. I look forward to heaven where there will be no more separations. I know thousands of people see their children go off to college, but for us it was much harder. The kids couldn't come home for summers and vacations.

Bill and I went back on the road to report to our churches and to visit new ones.

Stranded in the Mountains

Our diesel engine had been showing symptoms of being sick. We were traveling in West Virginia and we were praying that the engine would last until we got to Ohio. It took its last couple of breaths and died just as we topped a hill in a mountainous corner of Maryland. We were in the country, and as we quickly scanned the area, we saw an old garage with a sign, "We Repair Diesels." Bill was able to steer the car down the hill, and pulled it into the front yard of the garage.

There were no cars around, and the door was locked. There was a house a few yards away on the same side.

I said, "Let's go over to that house. Maybe the mechanic lives there, since there's nothing else around here."

We walked over, and knocked on the door. A pleasant lady – maybe in her forties – came to the door. She cautiously looked at us with a bit of suspicion.

"Hello. We are sorry to bother you, but we are missionaries and just traveling through. Our car died just as we came over that hill. We saw the sign on the garage that they repair diesel engines. Is the mechanic here?" Bill explained.

She seemed to relax when he told her we were missionaries. "No, he doesn't live here. Please come in, and I will try to call him on the phone."

We sat down while she tried to call the mechanic, but she couldn't reach him. "Well, my husband will be home soon. You are welcome to stay for dinner, and we will keep trying to contact Harold (the mechanic)."

"Oh, thank you so much. We certainly appreciate your hospitality, but we don't want to be a bother to you." I replied.

"It's no bother at all. I am just glad we can help you. There are no other people who live close to here. I am so glad the Lord let you break down here near us. My husband, Ron, and I are Christians also, and we attend a little Baptist church in town."

"Really? We are Baptist missionaries to Kenya. We have just come from a mission conference in Virginia, and we are on our way to Ohio to visit a church there."

Her face just beamed with the joy of the Lord and happiness that the Lord had given her the opportunity to minister to us.

We got acquainted with Sally while we were waiting for her husband to come home from his job in a coal mine. It was quite apparent that Sally loved the Lord with all her heart. I was thanking the Lord for the privilege of meeting her, even if we had to do it through the car trouble. I knew I really liked her, but I didn't realize then why the Lord had planned this meeting.

We felt an immediate kinship to Ron when he got home. He was as nice and friendly as Sally, and insisted we stay for dinner. He was able to get in touch with Harold, and he and Bill walked over to the garage to meet him.

Ron said, "Harold is a good mechanic, and he specializes in diesel engines, but he is a little weird. Don't be surprised at his personality. He is not a Christian, and we have tried to be a good neighbor, and to be a testimony to him. But we have had our difficulties in the past. We live so close, but we usually just try to stay out of his way. I sure hope he will be willing to help you."

Harold was living at the back of the garage. Ron knocked on his door, and he came to the door. Bill said he looked like an image of a mountain man that is portrayed in some movies. He was over six feet tall, and weighed around two hundred pounds. His grey hair was down over his ears and needed to be combed. His long grey beard was shaggy and unkempt. His eyes looked a little unfriendly as he spoke to Ron, and eyed Bill with curiosity.

"Harold, this is Bill Cunningham. He's a missionary, and he and his wife are just traveling through. His diesel engine died. Can you take a look at it?"

He seemed happy to be able to make a buck, so he said, "Sure. Where is the car?"

"It's in front of the garage. He was able to coast it down the hill and into the parking area."

The three men walked around the garage to the front. Harold unlocked the door and they went in. He immediately started to move around boxes of old car parts, tools, and junk to clear a place so they could pull the car in for him to check it.

Bill opened the hood, and Harold checked the engine. "I'll have to remove the heads, and you'll have to take them into town to a machine shop to see if they are cracked. I don't have the equipment here to check them."

He removed the heads. It was already too late to take them to town. "We can't do anything else tonight." We were left in a desperate position.

Bill and Ron then walked back over to Ron's house where I was visiting with Sally while she prepared dinner. When they came in, they explained to us what was going on.

Sally said, "You are welcome to spend the night with us tonight, and then I will drive you into town tomorrow."

"Oh, Sally. Are you sure you don't mind? We feel terrible to impose on you. You don't even know us. Is there a motel in town where we can stay?" I asked.

"No, I will not take you to a motel, because you are staying with us. The Lord let you break down right by our house, so we could help you." Ron was in full agreement.

"Thank you so much. We really appreciate it."

"You are welcome. Now, we have church tonight (it was Wednesday). You are welcome to go with us, or you can stay here and rest. It's up to you."

Bill and I immediately agreed to go to church with them.

The church attendance was about fifty people that night. Ron and Sally introduced us to all the people and the pastor, and they were very friendly. The pastor had special prayer for us during the service. He also told us there was no place close to buy an engine. He and Ron said the nearest place would be Pittsburg, Pennsylvania.

The next day Ron went to work, and Sally drove us into town with the heads which Harold had removed from the engine. After having them tested, we were told the sad news. They were cracked and finished. The engine could not be repaired. It would require a new engine.

We didn't know what to do. "*Lord, we don't understand this,*" we prayed. "*Surely you have some purpose in letting the engine be ruined, but we don't have the money for a new engine. We need your help. Please give us wisdom to know what to do, and supply our needs for this car.*"

Ron and Sally insisted we stay with them until we could get the car repaired. We had a church meeting scheduled in Ohio for the next Sunday.

Bill said, "We'll just have to call and cancel the meeting."

Ron quickly said, "Don't cancel your meeting. You can use my car to go to it." His car was a brand new Ford.

"Are you kidding? I can't take your new car. You don't even know me," Bill argued.

"The Lord has told me its okay. You take my car and go to your meeting."

We knew a pastor in Pittsburg, Rev. Billy Barrs, who was a long time friend and one of our supporting pastors.

Bill called him. "Hello, Billy, this is Bill Cunningham."

"Hey. Good to hear from you. How are you and LaMoin? And where are you?"

"We are both fine, and we are down here in Maryland. We have a problem. We hate to ask you, but we need your help." Bill explained to him about the car, and that we were going to Ohio for Sunday morning, but we would return Sunday night.

Billy replied, "I will be there on Monday. You can come up here, and visit with Janet and me. I have a mechanic in the church that can help us to find an engine for the car."

"Thanks so much. We don't know what we'd do without you. See you on Monday."

We left on Saturday to drive up to Ohio in Ron's new car. We prayed that nothing would happen to us on that trip. We couldn't believe he would trust us with his new car, and we certainly didn't want anything to happen to it. These strangers had taken us in like we were family. We were so grateful. God does direct our steps.

We had the meeting on Sunday, and drove back to Maryland that afternoon. We attended church with Ron and Sally that night.

Billy arrived around noon on Monday, and we drove to his home in Pittsburg. I was happy to be able to visit with Billy's wife, Janet – the Matron of Honor in our wedding. I had not seen her for a few years. We had a great time of visiting while the men went to look for an engine.

The mechanic took them to a place where they found a slightly used gasoline engine (which we wanted) and it had only 26,000 miles on it. Billy said his church would buy it for us. That was a huge blessing, because we didn't have the money to pay for it.

We wanted to get our car repaired as quickly as possible, so we left the next day. A man from the church put the engine in his truck, and followed us to Maryland. They unloaded the engine in Harold's garage, with the assurance from him that he could do the work of putting it into the car. Billy even told Bill that his church would pay for Harold's labor.

Ron and Sally were so gracious to us, and we continued to stay with them while Harold worked on the engine. But the work was going slowly. Another week passed, and he had not finished. We were getting anxious. Ron and Sally wouldn't even let us pay them anything for food. We certainly didn't want to overstay our welcome, and take advantage of them.

Harold still had the car torn apart, and he didn't seem to be doing much. Bill would go over every day to check on it. One day, he was in the garage talking with Harold and Bill started talking about Jesus. Harold almost went crazy.

He was angry, and said, "I don't want to hear that kind of talk here."

His reaction, and his strange ways, convinced us he was probably demon possessed. We knew we had a big problem with him. He always had an excuse for not being able to finish the job. Finally, Bill and Ron told him they would take the car out of his garage, and pay him for the work he had already done. But, he wouldn't let them take the car.

Bill talked to some men at the church, and they said, "Harold is crazy, and he could be dangerous. We will call the sheriff, and tell him what is going on, and then have him to meet us there to remove the car."

We then called Billy in Pittsburg, and updated him.

He said, "Get that car out of there with the sheriff's help, and my mechanic and I will come down there and tow it back here, then he can fix it."

Bill appreciated his offer, but he really didn't want to have to tow it to Pittsburg. Some of the men from the church in Maryland offered to work on it.

The men and the sheriff came one night, and they all went over to the garage.

The sheriff said, "Now, Harold, we've come to take this car out of here. I want you to get all the parts together that belong to this man and put them in the car. I don't want to have any trouble with you, but this man has a right to remove his car, and I am here to make sure it is done peacefully. Now, you tell us how much he owes you for your labor – and I want it to be fair."

Harold was angry, but he didn't resist the sheriff. They pulled the car out and took it over by Ron's house and parked it. Bill paid Harold the money he asked for, and we didn't see him again. It was awkward since he lived so close to Ron. We apologized to Ron and Sally, and hoped Harold wouldn't cause them any trouble.

Ron said, "Don't worry about it. We never see him anyway. It's not like we were neighbors. He has always stayed to himself."

They pulled the car into Ron's garage. The men from the church came and did the work Harold had refused to do. He had not done the rewiring and some other things. After they finished with the work, Bill took it for a test drive, and it ran like a new car.

By the time we left, we had been with Ron and Sally for almost three weeks! During that time, Bill preached at the church, and presented our work. The church took us on for support.

We also became close to Ron and Sally. She told me I was the sister she never had. We corresponded regularly for the next three years while we were back in Kenya. During that time, she would occasionally complain of pain in her arms.

We had just returned from Kenya, on our following furlough, when she called to tell me she had been diagnosed with bone cancer. I was devastated! I really loved her. We had a kindred spirit. Then only a couple of weeks later, my phone rang on Thanksgiving Day.

"Hello,"

"Mrs. Cunningham, this is Becky (Sally's 17 year old daughter). I just wanted to tell you that Mom passed away this morning. I cooked our Thanksgiving dinner, and Dad was carrying Mom to the table to eat - and she died in his arms."

I couldn't believe it! She had just told me a short time before that she had cancer, now she was gone. I cried as if she had been a blood relative. We had shared so much together since that "chance" meeting in Maryland. In spite of all the problems with Harold, God had a purpose in our car dying at that particular spot.

A few months later, Becky called again. This time she wanted to ask Bill if he would perform her wedding ceremony. She also asked me to sing at her wedding.

She said, "Mom would be so pleased if she was here. I wouldn't want anyone but you to do the wedding." We both were overjoyed for the privilege of being included in such a memorable time in the life of my good friend's daughter.

My Brother's Death

Three weeks before I learned of Sally's cancer, I received news that my brother was sick. He had passed out at work. It was first believed he had suffered a stroke. He was rushed to the hospital in Little Rock, Arkansas, and he remained unconscious for almost an hour. He was admitted for tests. After a week, the doctors told him he had a small malignant tumor on his lung which had metastasized to the brain.

His doctor said if they could kill the tumor on the lung, the one in the brain would die. He was prepped for radiation. He quickly realized they were preparing to give him full scalp radiation.

He asked the radiologist, "Why are you giving me radiation to the brain?"

"Didn't your doctor tell you what is wrong with you?"

"Yes, he said I have a tumor on the lung, and you are going to kill that one, so the one on the brain will die."

The radiologist couldn't believe it. "They have not told you the truth. I'm sorry to have to tell you this, but you have multiple tumors on the brain."

Marlin asked, "Will the radiation kill them?"

"No. Your condition is terminal. Set your things in order, because you only have about two months."

"Then why are you giving me radiation?"

"It will just make you more comfortable until the end."

"Then forget it. I'm not taking it. I have knowledge enough to know that when you kill cancer cells; you are going to kill good brain cells. If I am going to die anyway, I want to keep all of my mental faculties until I die."

Marlin went back to his doctor, and asked, "Why didn't you tell me the truth?"

The doctor replied, "I'm sorry. I just couldn't look you in the eye and tell you that you are dying."

My brother never took treatment, except Morphine for the excruciating headaches. He never complained. He suffered much – and died four months after the diagnosis.

My blood brother (who was saved), and my spiritual sister died three months apart. Most of you who are reading this can empathize with my feelings in losing these loved ones. But a greater sorrow was yet to come.

Through many experiences in my life, I have learned to practice (I Thess. 5:18), "In everything give thanks; for this is the will of God in Christ Jesus concerning you."

Chapter 22

A Fat Neck in Utah

Bill preached in a church in Utah on Wednesday night, and before the service, there was a prayer request for a man who was going into surgery for the removal of his cancerous thyroid gland. They said he had discovered it suddenly due to swelling in his neck. I was concerned for the man, and went back to the motel thinking about it.

The next morning we were dressing, and getting ready to leave for our next trip. Bill looked at me and said, "What's wrong with your neck?"

"Nothing. Why?"

"It's swollen."

"Get out of here. Quit trying to scare me."

"I'm not trying to scare you. It is swollen. Go look in the mirror."

I laughed as I walked to the mirror. One glance horrified me! My neck *was* swollen. It looked like a ring around the bottom of my neck about an inch wide. My hand automatically went to it. The swelling was slightly hard when I touched it. It wasn't sore – just swollen.

The prayer request the night before swiftly came to mind. "I haven't been bitten, so why is it swollen?"

"Well, I think we should see a doctor." Bill replied.

"We can't see one today. We've got to leave. When we get to Washington, maybe the pastor can recommend a good doctor."

When we arrived at the next church, it was still badly swollen. The pastor's wife called a doctor, and made an appointment for me.

The doctor examined it and said, "You have a goiter. I think you had better get to Mayo Clinic as soon as possible."

"Why? Is it that bad?"

"It could be. I can call and make you an appointment now."

"No. I can't go now. We have meetings scheduled that we can't cancel. I'll just have to wait until I get home in a couple of weeks."

"Where do you live?"

"Springfield, Missouri."

"Well, you'd better make sure you get a doctor who knows what he's doing and will follow through on this."

I left the office wondering if I would be requesting prayer for cancer. But I wasn't upset. Of course, I wondered what it could be, but God gave me peace about it. I knew whatever I faced; it was all under His control. We continued to travel to the churches where Bill was scheduled to preach.

Soon after our arrival in Springfield, I called the best doctor I could find. I was able to get in to see him quickly. He examined me, and confirmed it was a goiter. He scheduled several tests for me. We wondered what we were facing this time. We had come through many tears and trials. Were we facing another severe test of our faith and endurance? *Lord, when will we get some rest?*

In a few days I went back for the results of the tests.

"The goiter is a result of your inactive thyroid gland. It is barely producing. Your gland is like a muscle – the more you use it, the larger it becomes. Your thyroid gland has been working hard to produce the hormone which your body needs, and that's why it is has enlarged. You have what we call a "lumpy thyroid." There are many lumps in it, but no tumors and no cancer." I felt a huge relief.

"Will this goiter continue to grow?" My thoughts raced back to one of my high school teachers who had a goiter the size of a cantaloupe in her neck. It was so ugly, and it looked so uncomfortable. I always felt sorry for her, and wondered what caused it, and why it couldn't be removed.

"No. I am putting you on a thyroid replacement medication. You will have to take it every day for the rest of your life, but the medication will supply the hormone your gland has been trying so hard to produce. The goiter will go away."

I thanked the Lord for another deliverance of something which could have been serious. I have been taking the medication since then – except for a period of about two years. Isn't it strange that we take medicine to feel good, and then when we are feeling great, we think we don't need the medication any longer? Okay, so it's dumb, but I was guilty of doing it. I was amazed at all of the bizarre and painful symptoms which are produced by not taking the thyroid medication. I was a mess. I finally got my doctor book out, and I was astonished that all of my symptoms were the result of low thyroid.

I went to the doctor and told him what was wrong with me. Yes, I did. I made my own diagnosis. He accepted my diagnosis without much reaction, until the results of the test came back – the one I had requested.

The doctor called me at home. "I want you in my office STAT. Your thyroid is dangerously low. I must get you on medication. I must confess to you, I didn't pay much attention when you told me your symptoms, and what you thought was causing them. I hear those things every day. I shrugged it off.

Thank you for causing me to pay more attention to what people tell me."

I hope a lot of women were helped through that experience.

Chapter 23
Parting Was Not Sweet Sorrow

We, and the kids, celebrated Christmas together, and in January it was time for Bill and me to return to Kenya. I was dreading it. This would be the first time to go without our children. Wyvonna and Shaleen were living and working in Springfield, and Greg had transferred from Liberty Baptist University to Southwest Missouri State University in Springfield.

We rented a three bedroom apartment, so all of them could live together. During the few days before we left, we worked hard to get the apartment set up for them. We wanted everything to be as perfect as possible.

The day quickly came for us to say goodbye. The kids took us out to dinner the night before, and treated us to a wonderful meal. We rented a car to drive four hours to St. Louis, because the flights were much cheaper than from Springfield. On Sunday morning we were getting our luggage ready to leave, and the kids were getting ready for church. I was struggling. Saying goodbye to our friends, parents, and siblings in the past years was hard – but nothing compared to this. There are no words to describe my feelings.

I will have the image of that morning in my mind until God calls me home. We were all trying to keep from showing a lot of emotion, because that would make it worse. We hugged, kissed, and said goodbye. Bill and I walked out to the car which was parked in the parking lot in front of their ground floor apartment. I wanted to say, *"No, I cannot go without them."* But I knew I couldn't.

As we drove away, they were all three standing in the big living room window. Wyvonna was in her housecoat and had a towel around her head, because she had taken a shower and washed her hair. Greg and Shaleen were in their housecoats. They were not crying nor smiling as they waved goodbye to us. I waited until we drove out of sight, and then tears came in torrents. I cried half of the way to St. Louis. I have never felt more sorrow than I did that morning – not even at funerals of loved ones. Yes, missionaries do sacrifice, and that was the greatest sacrifice I will experience in working for the Lord.

We did not plan any stop-over during the flight. We were so sad; we could not have enjoyed any sightseeing. We were also tired from all the traveling and the work in preparing to leave America. We had packed and shipped a twenty-foot steel container filled with supplies for the field. It was tiring. We still faced a lot of work upon our arrival in Nairobi. We had to find a house, move into it, and go through all of the frustration of getting everything up and running for the house.

When we arrived in Nairobi, we were happy to see Simon and Carol, and some of the missionaries there to welcome us back. We went to stay with Jerry and Shari Piercey until we could find a house.

Ripped Off

We bought a car and started searching for a house. It was hard to find a nice one for the price we could afford. One day we met a Kenyan who was in real estate. He said he would help us to find a house. Of course, we would pay him a finder's fee, but it would be much easier to locate one with his help.

He called us, and said he had a house he would like to show us. We rushed to meet him. I was so eager to get into our own place and get settled. We followed him through the streets of Nairobi, turned off the main road, and drove through a small suburb. We then drove into an area where there were not any close houses. We drove to the end of the road, and saw the house. It was setting by itself on top of a small hill overlooking a valley.

I was not excited about the area, because in the event of trouble, it could have been dangerous. There was no way to escape except by the one narrow road. If the road was blocked, there would be no way out. However, I was impressed when I saw the large, pretty, two-story house. There was a high stone fence with large pieces of broken glass embedded in concrete on top. TIK. The guard opened the gate for us to enter, and we parked the cars and got out. The guard greeted our agent as an old friend, and gave him the key to the house.

We went inside, and walked through a pretty, modern kitchen, and then into a spacious dining room and living room. The floors were shiny wood and tile. Upstairs there were three large, airy bedrooms with beautiful views. There was a study room and two bathrooms. It was nice! It even had a built-in security system, but the wiring had been cut. Hmmmmm – no problem, we could fix it. We knew this was the type of house that was popular with the foreign government employees, but the foreigners would not have wanted it because of the risky location. The price was also acceptable. The agent told us we would have to pay a month's rent in advance and a month's rent for deposit.

We made the decision right then to rent it, and we drove back into the city to do the paperwork and pay the money. By that afternoon, we had a house! The agent even helped with getting the utilities connected.

The next day we made arrangements for a truck to deliver all of our household things which had been in storage while we were in the States. Our container would not be there for a few more weeks, but we had everything we needed to move in and set up our home. I was so relieved we did not have to look very long for a house, and I was excited to have such a nice one. The kids were coming over for Christmas, and I knew they would enjoy that place.

We moved into the house, and quickly had everything unpacked and set in order. I organized my kitchen, and put away my first supply of groceries that we had purchased a couple of days after we were in the house. We had even gotten a telephone in record time. Oh, such relief! We were settled and ready for another term of service.

We had been living there for about two weeks when a man knocked on the door. Bill answered the door.

I was in the background and heard the man say, "Hello. I am a representative of Mama Kenyatta (the wife of former President Jomo Kenyatta). I have come to inform you that you have no right to be in this house." *Uh-oh!*

"What do you mean? We rented this house from Mr. Joseph."

"He had no legal right to rent the house to you. He used to work for Mama Kenyatta, but he was discharged from her employ. He used to handle all of her properties, so he knows the houses and the guards. That is why he was able to show the house to you, but he had no right to rent it." TIK.

We were shocked and angry. We had been taken!

"Well, are you telling me we have to move?"

"Well, we can work something out with you, but you will have to rent the house from Mama Kenyatta."

"What about the money we have paid already?"

"I am sorry, but he has just taken your money. You will have to pay again to Mama Kenyatta."

We liked the house, and we were already established, so we didn't want to move. We knew we had been ripped off, but we were willing to deal with the crook later. We were going to go ahead and make a new deal with Mama Kenyatta.

"Okay," Bill told the man, "what do we have to do to make it legal?"

"Well, first of all, he was so anxious to make money from you that he didn't tell you the proper price for the rent. The real rent is $1,000.00 a month, with a month's deposit."

"What? That's twice what we paid for it."

"I am sorry. If you want to stay here, you will have to sign a contract for that much rent."

"No, we won't pay that much. Can't you lower the price? The house has been vacant for awhile. It's not worth that much money."

"That is the price. We cannot lower it. If you don't want to pay it, then you must leave."

We were devastated! And we were ready to hang that crooked little agent who had rented it to us. We knew his office. We would deal with him legally. He had cheated us out of $1,000.00, and put us into an awful mess. We had already moved all of our things, and now we had to find another house in a hurry.

We finally made a deal with the representative to let us pay a small amount of money for a couple of weeks until we could find another house. The search started again.

We were not happy, but God's word was still true – "And we know that all things work together for good….." (Romans 8:28). God knows the future, and maybe He was protecting us from being robbed and physically hurt. The house was in a secluded location which could have been a target for robbers. There were no close neighbors, so we could have been robbed and killed, and no one would have heard anything that was going on.

Besides, we had no choice. We were not going up against Mama Kenyatta!

When God Closes One House, He Opens Another

We drove through Runda, a housing area which was a few miles from downtown Nairobi. We loved the area. It looked almost like an American suburb. The houses were spacious with beautifully landscaped lawns. All of the houses had the necessary high stone walls around them, but the walls did not take away from the beauty of the area.

We really didn't have any hope of finding a house in Runda. It was a high rent area which was popular with foreign government employees whose house rent was paid by their embassy or other employer. But, we just wanted to see the area.

We turned off of Red Arrow Road – the road out of Nairobi which led to Kijabe – and into the main road of Runda. We drove down about a quarter of a mile, and saw a beautiful house with a sign out in front, "To Let," which meant "To Rent." I copied down the contact number - still thinking it would be impossible to afford it.

When we got back to Pierceys' house, I called the number. I talked to the owner and he asked if we wanted to see the house, and we agreed. In his sales pitch, he said he had been renting to the American Embassy personnel. There was a question in my mind - why had the Embassy taken it off of their home list? We made an appointment to look at it. Then I called the housing office at the Embassy. These people had the responsibility of finding houses for the government employees.

"May I speak to someone who can tell me something about a house which is for rent?"

"Hello, this is John Smith. May I help you?"

"Yes. I am a missionary, and I am interested in renting a house in Runda which used to be on your list for your employees. I would like to know why you are no longer putting your people in that house."

I told him the number and location of the house.

He said, "Well, it is a good house, and we rented it for a long time, but the owner refused to do some repairs on the place. We warned him about it, but he continued to procrastinate, so we removed him from our list."

"If you don't mind my asking - how much rent did you pay for it?"

"Let me check – hmmmm, looks like we paid $1,000.00 a month."

"Thank you. You have been very helpful."

We went to look at the house. We went through the front gate into a nice front yard with well maintained lawns, flowers, and shrubbery. There were thick, bougainvillea vines covering the high stone wall. The flowers on the vines were red and pink. I have always loved those flowers which grow profusely in Africa.

We entered the front door into a large foyer with beautifully polished wood floors. To the left was a room for an office and to the right was a guest bathroom. In front of us there were about four steps leading up to an open walkway. To the left was the living room with a fireplace (it gets cold in Nairobi), and in front of us was a spacious dining room. There were doors in the living room and dining room that opened onto a balcony with black wrought iron railings. At the end of the dining room was the large kitchen. We walked back down the steps to the entry where there was a stairway going downstairs. The house was built on a slight hill, so we entered at the ground level in front, and then the four bedrooms were on the lower level. The master bedroom had a large bathroom. There was a door which opened out onto the huge back lawn. Right in the center of the lawn was a palm tree! Perfect!

We loved the house, but I thought, *why are we tempting ourselves? We can't afford this.*

We tried not to show our excitement when we asked the scary question, "How much is the rent?"

The owner said, "I rented it to the American Embassy for $1,000.00 a month."

"Yes, but they stopped renting it, and removed it from their list of houses. They told us you would not make the necessary repairs."

"Oh, that has been done now." He proceeded to tell and to show us the things he had repaired.

We knew that to be removed from the American list was a big loss of business for him. Also, the other Embassies would be reluctant to rent it.

"We cannot pay that much."

After some hard negotiating, he agreed to our offer of $500.00 a month. Fantastic! He was in a financial pinch. He really needed to rent the house. I could hardly believe God had supplied the nice house for us. We began to thank God for the unpleasant experience with the other house – even the temporary loss of money.

We moved into the house, and lived there until we left Kenya.

There were many things about the house which I loved. One of the things was that beautiful palm tree in the back yard. I love palms!

One day as I was leaving, I asked our yard man to trim the tree, because it had some yellow, dead fronds on it. When I returned, and looked at my palm tree, I gasped! He had cut *all* of the fronds off except a few sticking up in the top! TIK. My beautiful palm tree was ruined! Well, I thought it was ruined. It took a long time for it to look normal. I felt like firing that gardener, but I decided to overlook it.

Chapter 24
He Stepped on My Last Nerve

When we returned from furlough, Mary was working for someone else, and there were other circumstances that kept her from coming back to work for us. I was disappointed, but I had almost learned to roll with the punches. Notice I said, "almost."

It was always difficult to find a good house worker who was experienced and trustworthy. *Most* of the workers took small things, like sugar and tea. That was to be expected, but I didn't want to be robbed.

It was a custom to write a reference letter for a worker when they left your employment. The next potential employer required a letter when they talked to a worker about a job. After hiring someone, you could quickly discover if their letter had been written by a former employer - or by a friend.

I hired one guy who truly had worked for a person from the American Embassy. Thomas spoke good English, and the letter praised his work. He was also supposed to be a cook – which was a plus for sure. The only trouble with him was he thought he knew more than I did!

One day I noticed Thomas had not run the vacuum cleaner. Most of the house had wood floors, but I had an area carpet in the living room. He had not worked for me long, so I was still instructing him on what I expected.

"Thomas, I want you to run the vacuum about every three or four days."

"Oh no, mama. If you run it too often, it will ruin the fibers in the carpet."

"You WILL run the vacuum when I tell you. Do you understand me?"

He reluctantly agreed. He just didn't want to do the work. He had been spoiled by the former employer. He felt he was not an employee, but was just my equal, and he didn't have to take orders – especially from a white woman. In other words, he was a smart aleck. He really pushed my buttons, but I needed him, so I let him survive.

We made friends with our Kenyan travel agent, and we invited him and his wife to dinner. Michael was educated and worked for the American Mennonite Travel Agency.

I cooked a wonderful meal and I had it all ready to put on the table, but Michael had not arrived. I tried to keep the food warm while we waited. Fifteen minutes passed, then thirty minutes, then forty-five minutes. After an hour, the food was getting cold, and I was hot! I have always been passionate about serving food when it is hot. One of the first arguments Bill and I had after we married was over his procrastination to get to the table when the meal was ready.

We sat down at the table, and I told Thomas to put the food on the table.

My servant said, "Oh, I say we wait for five more minutes."

Well, that was it! I had only one nerve left, and he stepped on it.

"Thomas, I didn't hire you to tell me what to do. You have the food on this table within the next two minutes, or you are sacked!"

He wasted no time in putting the food on the table. We were half finished with the meal when Michael and his wife walked in. I was furious! I know, to most of the Kenyans, that time meant nothing, but Michael was a business man. He had no excuse for being so late.

We later learned that Michael was also a crook! We paid him for airline tickets to the States. After we returned, the travel agency billed us for the money. Michael had been stealing money that customers paid, and he quit and started his own agency. TIK

Thomas didn't last long. I fired him shortly after that incident. I didn't pay him to cause me stress. I vowed I would never hire anyone else who had worked for American government employees. They came to the country for two years, and they were totally ignorant to the culture. They overpaid the workers and put them on equal level. Now, that might sound right to you – but it was not right in Kenya. In their culture, they were not on equal ground with their employers. If you trained them otherwise, you ruined them for living in their own culture. I know it is hard for you to understand, but you have to operate within the culture of a country. Otherwise, you are not even being fair to the people.

Chapter 25
Run Over by a Motor Boat

Bill was tired when we arrived back in Kenya. Then we had to move twice, which just contributed to his need for a rest. He is not a great fishing enthusiast, but our missionary friend, Jerry Piercey, came by the house and said, "Hey, Bill, you want to go fishing with me at Lake Naivasha tomorrow?"

"Oh, I don't think so, Jerry. I am just really worn out. I just need to rest."

"Well, you can rest out there while we drown a few worms. Or, if you don't want to fish, just set on the boat and relax in the sun."

I said, "I think it would be good for you to go with him. It is so beautiful on the lake, and he has that cabin boat. You could just set on the deck, and enjoy the scenery." Lake Naivasha is the second largest freshwater lake in Kenya, and is a part of the Great Rift Valley. It sets at an altitude of 6,180 feet. It's about eighty miles from Nairobi. It has an abundance of wildlife around it, and is home to a sizeable population of hippos.

We finally convinced Bill to go.

Jerry said, "Great. You will enjoy it. I'll pick you up about 4:30 in the morning."

I was up at 4:00 and as I stood in the kitchen preparing a lunch for Bill, the strangest thought entered my mind - *What if this is the last meal I ever prepare for him?* I was a little troubled by the thought, but then quickly released it from my mind.

I said goodbye to the men, then went back to bed for a couple of hours. Jerry's wife, Shari, was coming later in the morning to take me to see a doctor about some problems with my leg - the one I had injured when I fell down the stairs before our furlough.

She came, and we went into Nairobi. I saw the doctor; we had lunch, and then did some shopping. In the afternoon, she drove me home. When we got to my house, Boaz met us at the gate. He was a man we hired to live on the property to perform multiple chores – cutting the grass, trimming the hedges, caring for the flowers, and to open and close the gate for us or others.

I asked Boaz, "Is Bwana home yet?"

He turned his eyes downward and didn't answer me.

I asked him again with a bit more firmness, "Is Bwana home yet?"

He rolled his eyes, looked scared and asked, "Where have you been?"

He was making me mad. Where I had been was none of his business. He was my employee. He didn't have the liberty to question me about where I had been. As you can tell, patience is not my best virtue.

I became concerned, and I knew he was hiding something from me.

"Did Bwana come home?"

"Yes, but he left. They had a problem."

"What kind of a problem?"

He wouldn't answer me.

"Has there been an accident?" I asked.

"He nodded to indicate yes."

"Did they come here in the car?"

"Yes."

"Then the car wasn't hurt badly?" A boating accident didn't enter my mind.

He replied, "You have not received the report?"

"What report? Boaz, TELL ME what has happened. If you don't tell me now, I am going to sack (fire) you."

He really got nervous then. He still wouldn't answer me, but he went on the other side of the car, and told Shari the men had a boating accident, and Bill had been hurt.

Of course, I heard him. "Did they go to the hospital?" I asked.

He answered, "Yes."

We didn't have our phone in the house yet, (It took two months to get one, and then it went out every time it rained. TIK). We left immediately and went the short distance to Shari's house. I called the hospital, and learned Bill had been admitted.

We were on our way out the door when Jerry drove up. Jerry was a nervous wreck. Every time he started to tell us what had happened, he would almost start crying, and would have to stop talking. I was afraid he was going to have a heart attack. When he was finally able to talk, he explained what happened.

"We got into the boat when we first arrived at the lake, and went across the lake to Hippo Point. We anchored, and started to fish. Bill was sitting on the roof of the cabin. He had his legs stretched out with his feet against the little railing around the bow of the boat. We fished for awhile, but the fish weren't biting. We then decided to move on down the lake to another spot.

"I pulled the anchor up, and put it on the edge of the boat. Then I started the engine. I gave it too much gas, and the boat started to go too fast. Out of the corner of my eye, I saw the anchor start to fall. I quickly reached for the anchor, but it fell off and grabbed hold of the bottom of the lake, caused the boat to whip around, and Bill was thrown off.

"The engine died, and I kept expecting Bill to surface any moment. When he didn't, I walked around the boat looking for him and calling, 'Bill, Bill.' I walked the second time to the back of the boat by the engine. When I looked over, I saw the tips of his fingers on one hand. I thought he was dead! The water was too murky, and I couldn't see him. I jumped in, and started to feel for his body. Then I realized his shirt was tangled in the prop of the engine. I ripped his shirt off, got him loose, and pushed him to the surface. He regained consciousness enough for me to put his hands on the top of the boat. I told him to hold on while I got into the boat to pull him up.

"I finally pulled him up in the boat, and laid him down. He was bleeding a lot. He passed out again as I was speeding back toward the dock. I thought he had died. I tied the boat up, and the owner of the dock helped me to get him out. We laid him on the dock while I went to get the car."

We learned later that the dock owner was drunk. When he went back to the dock house, there were two teachers from Rift Valley Academy there.

He shook his head and told them, "Those missionaries had a bad accident, and Cunningham isn't going to make it. His head is split open, and you can see his brain."

His head was split open, but the skull was showing – not the brain. Thank God!

Jerry continued, "We got him in the car, and I took him to a little dispensary in Naivasha. The Indian doctor stitched him up. He had regained consciousness, but the doctor said he was going into shock. I left the dispensary and brought him to the hospital."

"LaMoin, I am so sorry. It was my fault. I almost killed him."

"Jerry, it was an accident. It could have happened to anyone. Just calm down or you're going to have a stroke or a heart attack. He will be okay."

Then the three of us drove into Nairobi to the hospital to see Bill. Before I saw him, the British doctor came to talk to me.

He explained, "He was hurt pretty bad, but he is stable now. He has bad lacerations on his head and back. When his friend brought him in, I examined him, and couldn't find a pulse or blood pressure. He was in shock. I thought we were losing him. I had to send for a specialist who was downtown. I really thought he would be dead before the doctor got here. He has swelling in his brain, and we are watching that. However, at this point we are more concerned about his lungs. He swallowed a lot of dirty lake water. It's a miracle he's alive." There were numerous, dangerous bacteria in that lake.

Jerry, Shari and I tried to determine how long he was under water. I timed Jerry as he acted out what happened after Bill went off the boat. The best we could figure, Bill had to have been under water for at least two minutes. It truly was a miracle he survived, since he was unconscious and breathing under water that long.

We went to the room to see Bill, and visited with him a short time. He was groggy, and we wanted him to rest.

On the way home, Jerry and Shari suggested I go to their house for the night. I quickly accepted their offer, because I just couldn't be alone at that time. They took me home, and I gathered the few things I needed for the night, and then drove my car to their house.

The next morning I drove home to shower and change clothes before going back to the hospital. I had locked my closet door the day before, and then could not find the key.

I searched my purse, my clothes, and everywhere I thought I could have put the key. I couldn't find it. I was almost frantic. Even though I had searched my purse, I dumped all of it on the bed. The key fell out!

I decided I would not lock the door. In my present state of mind, I was afraid I would lose the key again. I went into the closet, and laid the key on the shelf next to the door. I selected all of my clothes for the day, and laid them on the bed, and closed the door. I had not completely turned the lock around when I opened it then when the door closed, it locked! I had to get that door open. I tried to pick the lock with a hairpin, a nail file, and a small screw driver – without success. I could not get the door unlocked. Rats! I had to get to the hospital. I decided to worry about it later.

When I got to the hospital, I learned Bill had been released to go home. I questioned the wisdom of that decision, but – TIK. The doctor said he would have to have complete bed rest for a month. He could get out of bed only to go to the bathroom. I went to the hospital pharmacy, and filled his prescriptions for antibiotics and some other medication. Then I drove him home, and immediately put him in bed.

He wanted some fresh clothes and his house slippers – which were securely locked in the closet. My feet were aching from my high heels – but all of my other shoes were all safe behind that locked closet door! I didn't want to worry Bill, but I had to tell him about it. And true to a man's nature, he got out of bed, and tried to open the door – while I yelled at him. I finally forced him to get back into bed. Since I didn't have a phone, I drove over to Piercey's house to ask Jerry to come and get the door unlocked. He wasn't home! I left word with his house man for him to come as soon as he returned.

I went home and got a clothes hanger, straightened it out, made a hook on the end, and went fishing – for a key. I ran the clothes hanger through the louvers in the door, and tried to hook the key on the shelf. I succeeded in knocking it onto the floor. *Fine, there's an opening under the door, and I can fish it out.* I was down on the tile floor with my nose on the floor, trying to see under the door. I put the wire under the door - in and out, in and out. There wasn't even the jingle of that key.

I was already on my hands and knees, and feeling quite exasperated, so I gave up and prayed. *Please God. You know how my nerves are wrecked already with Bill's injury. Please help me get this wretched key out of the closet, so Jerry doesn't have to break the lock, or knock the door down. PLEASE, Lord.* Once more I slid the wire under the door, pulled it out, and with it came that naughty key!

Thank you, Lord, I prayed in a sigh of relief. He saved us the money of replacing the door.

Bill had to have complete bed rest, so I became his warden. Trying to force him to rest, after he was feeling better, was not an easy duty.

When he felt like talking, I got the rest of the story. He told the same story as Jerry up to the point of being thrown off the boat.

"When we agreed to move to another location, I reeled in my line, and laid the rod over my lap. I braced my feet against the railing and held on to the boat. I don't remember going off. Maybe my head hit the boat, and knocked me out. Then the engine pulled me into it. It cut my head, and shredded my back when my shirt got tangled up in the prop. I guess my body stalled the engine. The first thing I remember is waking up under the water, and I couldn't surface. I could see light above me, and I reached for the light. Jerry saw my fingers and jumped into the water. After Jerry put my hands on the edge of the boat, I remember saying, 'Get me out of here.'" It was amazing that Jerry walked to the back of the boat just as Bill reached up. That was God!

Jerry had a hard struggle to get Bill into the boat since Jerry is much smaller. When he helped Bill to lie down, Bill blacked out again. Jerry immediately headed the boat toward the dock at full speed. He thought Bill was dead.

"When I came to, my head was hurting. I pulled my handkerchief out of my pocket, put it on my head and said, 'Man, my head hurts.' Jerry gave a whoop and said, 'Thank God, you're alive!' Then I noticed I had blood all over me. I didn't know what had happened, because I was only half conscious."

Bill was conscious enough that he was able to get into the car with Jerry's help. The dock owner told Jerry about an Indian doctor at a small dispensary nearby, so he quickly drove to the dispensary. The doctor helped to get Bill inside. He said the doctor didn't look professional, and the office was dingy with bad lighting. Even in his condition, he noticed a bad odor in the room. The examining table was old and covered with a dirty sheet. Bill lay down on the table, and the doctor started to clean the wounds on his head. He first shaved the side of his head, and then he started to remove pieces of weeds and dirt.

The accident happened near Hippo Point, which is home to the largest population of hippos in Africa. The hippos spend their days wallowing in the mud and water to keep cool. They do not eat meat, thus they leave the water only at dusk to feed on the grass. An adult hippo weighs around four thousand pounds and can consume 150 pounds of grass each night. Except for feeding, everything else in their lives is done in the water.

Hippos have long, thick, razor-sharp teeth or tusks. They are capable of biting a small boat in half, and they kill more people every year in Africa than any other animal. They are vicious and will attack. We couldn't understand it, but were thankful the dangerous animals were not present when the accident happened. God was there!

Because of the hippos, the water was dirty. Bill's wounds had to be thoroughly cleansed. It was painful to have the wounds cleaned without any medication, but after the doctor cleaned them, he started to sew them up. Bill said it really hurt, and it sounded like ripping cardboard. He would draw his head back when the needle went in.

The doctor said, "You're going to have to be still."

"Would you like to change places with me?"

Bill heard the doctor say to Jerry, "I cannot give him a shot, because he is going into shock – it would kill him."

When the doctor had finished the torture, he wrapped an old dirty blanket around Bill, collected the money for his services – and for the blanket. Jerry and Bill got into the car, and began the 80 mile drive over the mountain to Nairobi. The roads were not paved, and they were filled with pot holes, but Jerry made the trip in about an hour. He was still afraid Bill would die of shock. He had to get him to Nairobi Hospital.

Our house was on the road going into the city. When they got to our area, Bill told Jerry to go by the house.

"I've got to get you to the hospital."

"I'm not going to the hospital in these dirty clothes filled with blood. I've got to get some clean clothes." He was in shock.

Bill insisted, so Jerry drove to the house, and helped Bill to get into some clean clothes.

When they left, Bill told Boaz, "If you tell mama what has happened, I will fire you. Do you understand?"

"Yes, Bwana."

That is why Boaz was afraid to tell me about the accident. Bill had told him he would be fired if he told me, and then I told him I would fire him if he didn't tell me. I was impressed with his quick thinking.

News traveled fast in Kenya. Since the RVA teachers had been at the lake, the rumor mill was running at high speed – Bill was either dead or dying. I was so afraid the news would quickly get back to the States by someone, and then the kids would hear it. I finally decided I had to call them.

I got them all on the phone and explained about the accident. I quickly assured them their Dad was going to be fine.

The next day Greg called, and asked, "Mom, are you sure Dad is okay? We thought he might have an arm or something cut off, and you're not telling for fear you'll upset us. But we want to know the truth."

I assured him I had told them the whole story, and Bill was going to be just fine.

The doctor told me Bill must stay in bed for at least a month, because of the swelling in his brain. *What? Did he realize how difficult that assignment was going to be?* I had my work cut out for me. It was going to take the power of God to keep him in bed for a month. Sure, he had been tired, but he always bounced back quickly, and was ready to get back to work. This was going to be a challenge.

I was preparing breakfast the morning after I brought him home from the hospital. I had purchased eggs on the day of the accident, and told my new house boy to wash them, and put them in the refrigerator. (Eggs were never washed before they went to market, and they were usually dirty.) I looked everywhere in the fridge, and I couldn't find them. I asked him where they were, and he showed me – in the freezer! TIK.

After a few days, it was impossible to keep Bill in bed. One day I told him I had to go into town to run some errands.

"I'm going with you."

"No, you're not. You know what the doctor said. You must have bed rest."

"I've had all the rest I need. I've got to get out of this house for awhile."

I couldn't talk him out of it, and I wasn't big enough to restrain him. He did consent to letting me drive, since he had orders from the doctor he was not to drive for at least a month. It was always difficult for him to ride as a passenger in the car. He trusted my driving, but he just always wanted to drive.

I was still a bit nervous about the whole experience of the accident, and still concerned about the long term effect of the injury to his head. The doctor was also still concerned about his lungs. His voice was hoarse, because of the water in his lungs.

We were going into the city, and I gave my signal to make a right turn (we drove on the left.) Just as I started to turn, the dummy in the car behind me decided to pass me, and he slammed into my front fender. TIK. *Oh, please, Lord. Bill has a head injury; he shouldn't be out of bed, and now we've had an accident. What next?* I was worried about the impact of the car hitting me, because it was on Bill's side. He didn't need any more blows to the head, nor did he need this stress to complicate matters.

We did the normal thing – got out and yelled at the other driver! The damage was minor, and Bill seemed to be okay. After some discussion with the other driver, we continued on to Nairobi.

Bill tried to rest the remainder of the month, but it was hard for him. He felt he had too many things to do. It was a stressful time, but he progressed well, and the doctor eventually thought he was well enough to get back to normal activities.

He gave me a scare a few months afterwards. We were in the car, and he was driving. He knew the area well. We stopped at a crossroad, and he just sat there. Finally, he asked, "Which way do I turn?" *Oh, no, is this the result of his head injury?*

He said later he had just blanked out for a minute. It never happened again.

Chapter 26
Capitol City Baptist Church

We continued our work with the Indians, but we had the burden to start an international church. There were thousands of English speaking people in Nairobi from other countries, and no one was trying to reach them. There was no English speaking church for them to attend. We felt we could incorporate these folks into our Indian work.

We needed to find a building to rent where we could have church services. Property was expensive to buy in Nairobi, and we had no money. We searched all over the city for a house, school, or some kind of an appropriate building to rent.

The Sarit Shopping Center had just been completed a short time before. It was near the Westland's Shopping Center. It was not anything compared to our malls in America, but there were many shops in this large multi-storied building - including a decent grocery store. The stores were clean, and all of them were grouped together in the one large building, so most of the expatriates were going there to shop. On the second floor was a nice Indian restaurant. Since we loved Indian food, we went there for lunch one day.

After lunch, as we were leaving the restaurant, we looked across the walkway and saw a large vacant room which appeared to be a conference room with nice chairs and a sound system. Maybe this was the answer to our need for a place to have church services.

We went back to the restaurant, and asked the Indian owner about the room. He said it belonged to him, and it was seldom used unless they had a large reception. We explained to him about our church, and asked him if he would consider renting it to us for meetings on Sundays. We felt happy and relieved when he agreed. We were even happier when he quoted a reasonable price, and agreed he would never rent it to anyone else on Sunday.

We put out advertisements all over the shopping center about the meetings. Soon people started coming. We had the beginning of our international church with a variety of nationalities - Indians, Canadians, Africans, Americans, British, and others.

The Bank Guard

One day Bill was at our bank near the Sarit Center, and he started talking to one of the Kenyan bank guards about coming to church. The man was interested and agreed to come the next Sunday, which he did. He made friends quickly in the church. Before long, he made a profession of faith, and was baptized.

After some time, Peter came to me one Sunday before church started. We talked for awhile, and he told me he felt God was calling him into the ministry. He expressed he was going to quit his bank job, and start a church in one of the slum areas. He seemed so burdened for that particular area, but I advised him not to quit his job. Good jobs were hard to find in Nairobi. Later he spoke to Bill about it, and asked if the church would fund him to start a church there. Bill told him he would have to prove himself first.

Bill said, "If you are serious about working for the Lord, then you can attend services here on Sunday, and then go out there, and teach a class in the beginning. In the meanwhile you can get some more training." He agreed with Bill.

For a few weeks, he would come to church, and tell us what great results he was having in his new class. He even gave us a report of the money the people had contributed to the work.

The man seemed so serious and dedicated. I tried to get Bill to put him on a small salary, and to help him with the expenses of the work he was doing. Bill still didn't trust him. I was getting annoyed with Bill, because the man seemed to be doing so much without any help.

One Sunday, he told us he could not be in church the next week. He had to accompany some government officials on a trip, and act as a body guard.

He didn't come back to church for about a month. Finally, one Sunday morning, Peter came to church. He appeared weak and walked with difficulty. As he walked, he would hold his side with one hand. Naturally, we were all concerned about him. Bill asked him if he was sick.

"Oh, Bwana, a terrible thing happened. There were two cars which went on the trip I told you about. There were three other guards besides me. We were traveling at night in the mountains, near the escarpment. Some bandits blocked the road. When the cars stopped, they came with guns. They took all the money from the important men. When we tried to stop them, they started shooting. I was the only one who escaped, but they shot me in the side. God was watching over me. I managed to crawl away and hide, then when they were gone, some kind people came along in a car, and found me. They brought me to the hospital in Nairobi, and I have been there until now. I had to have an operation to remove the bullets, and I have been sick since that time. I almost died. I have a large hospital bill, and I have no way to pay it."

A Canadian couple heard this story, and had such pity for this poor man. We did not know at the time, but they later gave him $300.00 to help with his expenses.

He came back to church the next week. He was still holding his side, and appeared to still be in pain when he walked.

Bill had some doubts. I was beginning to have a couple of doubts also. Bill asked some people at the bank about it. They laughed. There had been no shooting.

The next Sunday, Bill called the man outside. "You must have a terrible wound from the bullets and the surgery."

"Oh, yes, Bwana, it's bad." He opened his shirt and showed Bill a large bandage.

"I want to see where the bullets went in."

"Oh, I cannot open the bandage. It might get infected."

"No, we will just open it, and close it quickly." Bill finally pulled the bandage back from his side. His side was completely uninjured. There were definitely no wounds! Bill sharply reprimanded him. Afterwards, we never saw him again. TIK. It was such a waste. As an actor he could have received an academy award!!

Chapter 27
We Rescued the Captive Americans

There were few dull days in Kenya. Life was so different, and something unexpected was always just around the next corner.

One day we went to the Hong Kong Restaurant to eat. They had the best Chinese food in Nairobi. So many of the expatriates went there, and we usually always saw someone we knew.

The restaurant was full, and we were just finishing our meal when we noticed two couples at a table near us. They were speaking English, and they didn't appear to be locals. After we finished, we went to their table, and introduced ourselves. They were from Dallas, Texas, and they had been in Kenya about two months. They were not happy campers.

We seemed to make friends immediately, and they told us a disturbing story. They were in the construction business in Dallas. One Sunday a Kenyan man had spoken at their church. After the service, they were talking to him. He learned they were building contractors. He became excited, and presented a plan to them which would help his people, and also make money for them.

He said he and some of his friends in Nairobi were going to build a new housing development, but they needed money. He was persuasive in presenting to them that he had to have a large sum of money to get the government's approval. If they could put up the money, he and his partners could start the project. After much discussion, it was suggested that the contractors go to Nairobi, and build the houses. Then they would sell them and split the profits.

The deal sounded great and lucrative. The Americans were excited, plus they knew a man who could finance the project. They succeeded in convincing their rich friend about the wonderful business deal. Soon, the two American couples were off to Nairobi on the adventure of their lives – which would make them rich.

But, things didn't work out the way they had planned. TIK. They arrived in Nairobi eager to get to work, but instead, the Kenyan kept stalling them. They had already advanced the money to start the project – to prove to the government they were going to build the houses, which would enable them to get the permits they needed.

After about two months of wasting time and money, the Kenyan had taken them to a hotel to wait until he could get the deal on tract. He said he had to go on a short trip to Uganda, and they were to stay in the hotel until he returned.

"We don't know what is going on. We are almost out of money. He said he would pay for the hotel when he returns. We suspect something bad is going on. He forgot to take his briefcase, and he hasn't been back for a couple of days. We tried to check out of the hotel, but we were told we couldn't check out until he returns. We are frightened, but we don't know what to do."

Bill and I looked at each other with the same thoughts in our minds – *they were in big trouble!*

Bill said, "I think you've got to get out of that hotel. You can come to our house and stay until we can find out what's going on."

We took them back to the little hotel. They got their things together, and we started to leave the room. Bill grabbed the locked briefcase to take with us.

Jim asked, "What if they won't let us leave?"

Bill answered, "We're not asking or informing anyone. We are just walking out. There's nothing they can do.

We went back to our house. They were frightened by now. They were now convinced they were victims of a swindle of about $200,000.00, but they also feared for their lives.

Well, naturally, we wasted no time in breaking the lock on the briefcase to see what was inside. It was shocking! We found plans which indicated the Kenyans were in on a plot to assassinate Milton Oboto, the president of Uganda. We were convinced from the things in the briefcase that they were going to implicate these Americans. They had their passports, information and pictures. There were letters about plans to convince them to go to Uganda for some business. If the Americans were arrested, they would go to jail, and the Kenyans would be free of them - and keep the money. Dangerous stuff! They were actually holding them captive until they could get their plan to rolling.

We knew now we were all in danger. We didn't think anyone saw us leave the hotel, or followed us, but we didn't know for sure. They were afraid to get outside or even near a window.

We called their friend in America who had financed the deal, and he promptly came to Nairobi. He was angry about the money, but he was concerned for the safety of his friends. He just wanted to get them home before something happened to them.

We hid the three of them until they could make arrangements to return to America. In a few days, we took them to the airport, and they flew back to Dallas. Their lives were spared, but they went home broke.

We never heard anything else about it, and no one ever came looking for the briefcase. God protected our lives and the lives of our friends. It was scary and exciting, but I don't ever want to experience that kind of excitement again.

Chapter 28
My Job at the American Embassy

When the phone rings in the middle of the night, it usually is not good news. Because of the time difference between Kenya and America, the kids usually called in the middle of the night. When I answered the phone, it was Shaleen. Fear coursed through my body. *What's wrong? Has there been an accident?*

After she assured me she was okay, I began to breathe again. She wanted to come home – to Kenya. She was homesick, and things weren't going well for her. I woke Bill, and asked him what he thought about her returning. My decision was already made – of course, she was coming home. We told her we would start to work on getting the ticket for her, and we would let her know the details as soon as possible. Shaleen arrived in Nairobi in a few days. We were so happy to see her. She was happy to be home again. She knew that eventually she would have to return to the States, but she would stay through Christmas.

While we were making arrangements for her to return, I had an idea it would be good if she could get a job and stay in Nairobi for a while. I called the American Embassy and asked if they had any jobs that might be available. The person on the line said she had heard they needed an American to work in KUSLO – Kenya United States Liaison Office. KUSLO was the military liaison office which handled any military operations in Kenya. I asked to be transferred to the office.

"I was told you need a local hire in your office."

"Yes, our Navy Commander needs someone. I will get him on the phone."

Commander Lobbs came on the phone. I told him I was calling to try to get a job for my daughter, who was returning from the States. He then informed me that since she would not be a resident, she would not be eligible for the job. It had to be filled by a local American with a resident visa.

"Since we can't hire her, why don't you consider it?" he asked.

"Oh, no. I am a missionary. I am not looking for a job."

"At least come in, and talk to me about it. You might change your mind."

I finally agreed to go to talk to him. I had mixed feelings as I entered the Embassy. I went into the front entrance lobby, and walked past the Marine security guards to the receptionist, who was behind bullet proof glass.

"I have an appointment with Commander Lobbs."

"I will get you an escort."

Before my escort arrived, I went through the security check. They waved a wand over me, and searched my purse.

Soon the security door opened, and an American man motioned for me. He introduced himself, and we casually chatted as he took me to the third floor and down the hall to a security door with a push button combination lock. He knocked on the door. From inside, a voice asked for identification before opening the door. Only the top two floors had locked doors. KUSLO was on the third floor, and the offices of the Ambassador were on the fourth floor.

I walked into the office, and was greeted by a secretary at a desk across the room in front of me.

"Hi, I'm Barbara. I will get Commander Lobbs."

I looked to my right, and saw a large room with four desks. To the right of that room was another room with two desks. There were men at each desk in civilian clothing. Commander Lobbs came from my left, greeted me with a handshake, and asked me to follow him to his office. He was also dressed in civilian clothing.

I followed him down a short hall where I first saw a small coffee room on the right and a larger office straight ahead. We walked into his office – the second door on the right. He immediately put me at ease, and we talked about the job and my qualifications. He needed someone who could be his assistant. The job would require me to do some typing and filing, but mostly assist him with foreign visitors in the office, be able to help trouble shoot at the Consulate in Mombasa during the visit of our navy fleets, and to secure aircraft clearances for our military planes. I would also have to arrange emergency medical evacuations for any injured personnel while they were serving or visiting in Kenya.

He explained the office was manned by the Army Commanding Officer – Colonel Malloy, an Army Major, an Air Force Colonel, an Air Force Tech Sergeant and himself. On board also were Colonel Malloy's secretary that I had met in the front office and the Commander's present assistant who was returning to the States - and whose job I would be filling. There would be various teams of US military personnel in and out of the country on TDY – temporary duty. We had no bases in Kenya – just KUSLO. The governments had agreed to a low military profile. That explained why no one dressed in uniforms.

He was pleased with my qualifications, and offered me the job. I told him I was not at all sure I could take it. I would have to discuss it with Bill and others and pray about it.

"Okay, I'll tell you what. I have to leave tomorrow and will be gone for two weeks. When I return, I will call you. If you want the job, it's yours."

I agreed to let him know my answer when he returned.

I did pray every day about the job. Bill and I discussed it, and agreed there was nothing in our mission's rules which stated I could not work, even though it would be an unusual thing. We finally felt it was okay with our mission rules and God if I took the job. Of course the money would be helpful, and I had free time. It would not interfere with my duties as the wife and helper of a missionary. We felt that it might be God's will to help to reach the government workers. Most of them were lost, and no one was trying to witness to them. I also prayed that if God didn't want me to take it, the Commander would not call back. But when he returned, he called me, and I accepted the job.

I must admit that I did feel pretty important. It was a great opportunity. I immediately acquired a lot of prestige. I felt good when I could flash my identification at the desk upon entry, and the locked doors opened for me. I no longer had to identify myself when I reached the locked door at KUSLO – I just punched in the security code.

They issued me a two way radio to keep in my home. Every morning as I dressed for work, we listened to the roll call of the Embassy employees.

"LaMoin Cunningham, do you read me?"

I would reply, "I read you loud and clear."

It gave us a secure feeling to know if trouble came in the country, the Embassy had our backs. We laughed many mornings when the roll call was given. Only one man was determined to use proper English when he answered, "I read you loudly and clearly."

My Job at the American Embassy

The job also insured more security for all of our missionaries if an evacuation was ever necessary. I would be right there in the office that was responsible, and I could make certain that our missionaries were rescued. However, it created some problems with some of the missionaries. When I was hired, Commander Lobbs made it very specific that I was not to use the Army Post Office for anything or anyone other than my family. Later some of the missionaries asked me to let them mail things to my APO address for them to avoid customs. I had to refuse - which created some hard feelings with the missionaries. However, I felt that since I had made a promise about the APO that I would be deceitful and that if I was ever caught, it would be a terrible Christian testimony. My conscience would not permit me to let them use my APO address. I still feel that I made the right decision, even though they were angry with me.

During my first week, some of the guys teased me about being a preacher's wife. "Oh, no – she's a preacher's wife? She will be trying to convert us. She will be preaching to us."

I told them, "I will never bring up the subject of church, the Bible, or religion unless you initiate it. But if you ask me questions, then I assure you I will talk about it."

Those military officers showed me only kindness and respect. I have never worked with a nicer group of people. They never used bad language around me, and they never made any inappropriate passes. Nevertheless, after I was in the office for awhile, many of them did bring up the subject of the Bible. I had many opportunities to freely witness to them. I will never know until I get to Heaven how much influence I had on those men, but I know they all heard the gospel at various times. They even showed great interest. They never laughed at me, or scoffed about the Bible. I enjoyed every day of my work there – well, *almost* everyday.

I had many opportunities to get acquainted with the men – mostly officers – who came into the office during a three month TDY. I gave the gospel to many of them.

My job required me to have a secret security clearance, because classified information always came across my desk. Commander Lobbs was getting agitated because my clearance had not been granted from the States. Maybe it was taking longer because I had lived in so many foreign countries. There is much investigation and expense required in securing a secret clearance.

During this time, we had an Army General from the Southern Command in Florida to visit Kenya. Commander Lobbs was out of the country, and it was my responsibility to secure the clearances for our aircraft to land. I had to follow protocol, and deal with one certain man in the Kenyan government. On this particular day, we had a military plane coming in that was loaded with perishable supplies. They were transporting the supplies to another country, but it was a necessity for them to land in Nairobi. I had tried for hours to secure the clearance, and my Kenyan contact was showing no intention of giving me the clearance. Sometimes it made him feel good and important to be difficult. TIK.

Finally, I went into Colonel Malloy's office. He and the General were casually talking.

"Please excuse me. Colonel, I need your help." I explained the situation to him.

"Sir, do I have your permission to go over my Kenyan contact's head to get this clearance?"

"Do whatever you have to do."

"Thank you, sir."

I then went to the top man in the Kenyan government office. I told him the urgency of the situation, and immediately he assured me the clearance would be approved. I told him I would stay in the office until he notified me it had been granted. All the staff except Colonel Malloy and the General left the office at 5 o'clock. I stayed and waited for the "all clear" on the clearance. The plane was getting closer and closer to Nairobi. They kept stressing the importance of getting that landing clearance. I was still in the office when the General and Colonel Malloy left for the day.

Colonel Malloy asked, "Why are you still here? It's after quitting time."

"I'm staying until I have secured that landing clearance." After a short time, the clearance was granted. I notified the plane's pilot that he had been cleared to land.

I left the office, went downstairs and met Bill. Just as we were walking down the steps of the Embassy, the General quickly walked up beside Bill.

"Your wife is one h_____ of a worker. I'm impressed with the job she did." Then he looked at me and said, "If you ever return to the States and need a job, contact me."

A few days after the General returned to America, my secret clearance was approved. Hmmmmmm. Did the General have something to do with that?

Bill and I Helped to Rescue the Navy

One day a couple of enlisted sailors came into the office needing help. I talked with them.

"We have been to the States on furlough. We were heading back to Diego Garcia to report for duty, but our military plane has broken down here in Nairobi. There are ten of us. We have no money, and we have maxed out our credit cards. We don't have a place to stay or any way to buy food. We don't know when the plane will be repaired. We need help." I appealed to all the officers in the office, but they had no sympathy.

My boss said, "There's nothing we can do."

I said, "What do you mean? These are American sailors. They are stranded in a foreign country. Surely we can offer them some kind of accommodations."

"They are not my responsibility."

"Well, they can't go hungry, and sleep on the street."

The reaction from all of them was, "I'm not taking them into my home."

I called Bill and told him the situation. We had a big house. Only the two of us lived in it at the time.

"Bill, do you mind if I invite these guys to stay with us?"

"Not at all. I will come in and pick them up."

Bill came in, picked them up, took them to the house, and made some food for them. They stayed with us for three days before their plane was repaired. They were nice guys, and they appreciated what we did for them. However, I took a lot of razzing in the office.

"Why, there's nothing those guys won't do. You'll be lucky if they don't rob you. That bunch of thugs would do anything. I would never let them stay in my house." They had their jokes and laughs.

A few days after the sailors left, I received the nicest letter from their Commanding Officer on "the rock" (Diego Garcia). He thanked me for taking in his men when they were stranded in a foreign country. He heaped on the praise. Colonel Malloy read the letter and made the notation on it, "Good job, LaMoin."

We Met the Fleet

A Navy fleet of ships was due to dock in Mombasa. Commander Lobbs had to be there to meet it. He told me he

My Job at the American Embassy

wanted me to go with him. He said KUSLO would pay my expenses, and Bill could go with us.

We stayed at a nice hotel in Mombasa. The Commander would go out to the ships, while I stayed in the office at the Consulate to take phone calls from Nairobi, or to carry out any orders from him while he was on the ships. Of course, part of our job was to trouble shoot for any problems with the sailors while they were on shore leave. When you have 5,000 sailors on shore leave after months at sea, you are likely to have problems.

One sailor was injured on one of the ships. They were testing some of the big guns on one ship, and he happened to be standing too close. He was hurt, and we thought for awhile I would have to arrange for a medical plane to come from our base hospital in Germany, and transport him for treatment. It turned out his injuries weren't serious enough to go to Germany, and he received treatment from the medical crew on the ship.

One night, the Consular gave a big party for the official staff of the Consulate and the officers on the ships. Bill and I were invited. Commander Lobbs said he might need a driver after the party - which he did. It was quite a lavish garden party. All of the important people were there. We were welcomed, and included in all the introductions and mingling. I have never seen a spread of food like I saw there. It was all quite exciting. Many people only had a social drink, but my boss drank a little too much to drive back to the hotel. He knew he could depend on Bill to drive, so he took advantage of the situation.

We did not hesitate to let the people know we were missionaries, and that I was employed by the Embassy. I hope God used our testimonies to impress someone there that we were serving someone higher than our American government.

After we returned to Nairobi, a sailor was brought to our office. He had been out "looking for his roots" and failed to be on the ship when it left. It was a costly mistake. Leroy had his stripe removed, had to pay for the helicopter which flew him back to his ship, and was immediately put on cleaning detail – besides being cussed out.

I had many great experiences in that job. Bill was made "Honorary Chaplain" by the Ambassador. He performed a wedding for one of the Marines, and we were invited to the Embassy parties - especially the military parties with the Ambassador and the other high ranking officers in the Embassy. At first, we debated about going, but then we decided the Lord could use our testimonies before those people who were lost, and had no one trying to witness to them. They knew when we went to their parties that we would drink a coke, interact with people, and then when the liquor started to flow, we would excuse ourselves and leave.

We attended the promotion party for a colonel one night. He was a nice guy. He said, "This is the last promotion I want."

"Why?" we asked.

"Because I heard that all generals have aids." (Assistants – not AIDS.)

On a slow day in the office, the Air Force Colonel started a conversation with me about the Bible. He asked me a couple of questions, and I answered them. As a result, I sat in his office for about two hours witnessing to him. He didn't make a profession of faith to my knowledge, but God says his word will not return void. I pray he used the scriptures I gave that man to later convict his heart. I may see him in Heaven.

Some of them came to our church. We didn't always see visible results, but we know the Lord used us in their midst. After two years, that chapter closed in my life, and the time came for me to move on to other things the Lord had for me. I will always remember those days at the Embassy with pride, appreciation, and thankfulness for the opportunity God provided for me.

My Job at the American Embassy

Much later, on August 7, 1998 I was shocked and saddened when Bin Laden's terrorists bombed the Embassy. The KUSLO offices overlooked the parking area at the back of the Embassy – where the truck loaded with explosives exploded. The bomb ripped through KUSLO, and killed some of the people I worked with, and others that I saw every day. When I was working in the Embassy, we knew we were probably under surveillance, but never dreamed of the horrible devastation which happened in the future. God had me there for a season, and then moved me out to protect my life.

Chapter 29
Bad News from Home

My dad had been suffering with Alzheimer's disease for a few years. He was getting difficult for my mother to care for him, but she refused to put him in a nursing home. One day the phone rang. I answered it, and it was my mother. She told me my dad had been admitted to the hospital, and the doctor said he could not recover. He didn't recognize anyone, and he was almost non-responsive.

"Mother, I will come home as soon as I can make travel arrangements."

"No, the doctor said it is better for you not to come at this time, because he could remain like this for weeks or months. You might come home and have to return before he dies. There is nothing you can do, and he will not know you. Just wait for a while until we feel it is time for you to come."

"Okay, but you let me know as quickly as possible when I should be there."

A couple of weeks later, I called her to see how dad was doing, and how she was coping. She started to cry.

"Mother, even if Dad doesn't need me and won't know me, I think you need me now."

Through her tears, she said, "Yes, I do. I'm staying in the hospital most of the time, and I am worn out. I do need you here with me." "Okay, I will be on my way as soon as I can get a ticket."

I left Nairobi the next day. Wyvonna and Greg were living in Springfield, Missouri so I flew there so they could drive me to my mother's home in Arkansas. I arrived at night after the long trip, and I was exhausted. I went to bed soon after I arrived. Early the next morning I called my mother before seeing Wyvonna.

"How is Dad?"

"Didn't Wyvonna tell you?"

"Tell me what?"

"Your dad died yesterday." I was shocked. He died while I was in flight.

Wyvonna said, "You were so tired when you got here. I wanted you to get some sleep before I told you. There was nothing you could do last night."

Wyvonna, Greg, and I left that day to drive the four hours to my mother's home.

We went straight to the funeral home where they were having the viewing. I went first to my mother to grieve for a moment together. I greeted my brothers, and other relatives and friends, and then I walked over to Dad's casket. I looked at the body of flesh he had moved out of, and thought, *that is not my daddy. My daddy is enjoying a perfect mind and walking and talking on the streets of gold right now.* God gave me wonderful peace as I bent to kiss his forehead. As I stood looking at him, I thought, *Dad, you have just gone on this trip ahead of me. I couldn't go with you now, but I will meet you in Heaven.*

Mother Goes to Kenya

We buried Dad, and I started the task of taking care of all of the legal things which have to be done when there is a death.

Mother was a nervous wreck from caring for Dad for so long before he died. It had really taken a toll on her. I didn't feel good about leaving her by herself, so I suggested she return to Kenya with me. She consulted with my three brothers, and they agreed she should go.

We had some obstacles to overcome. She did not have a passport, and it would take about six weeks to make application and receive one by mail. I had already been home for awhile, and I couldn't be away from my job at the Embassy for another six weeks. God provided a solution. My cousin lived near Chicago. I called him and asked if he would drive us into Chicago to the passport office. He agreed.

We went back to Springfield, stayed for a couple of days, and flew to Chicago. My cousin met us at the airport, and we went to his home for the night. Early the next morning, he drove us into the city. We applied for her passport in the morning, and then we went to lunch, and did a bit of sightseeing. We picked her passport up just before the office closed in the afternoon.

We spent the night with my cousin, and flew out of Chicago the next morning. Mother had never flown, but she loved it. We stopped over in Amsterdam, and I took her for a boat ride on the canals, and we did some other sightseeing. She was tired, but she was seeing things she had only dreamed about.

Waiting for the Kill

Mother stayed in Kenya for four months, and really had the time of her life. She loved Nairobi. Shaleen was still with us, and she would take Mother into Nairobi and spend the day while I was working. She loved shopping in the big souvenir market and eating Chinese and Indian food. She had never experienced anything so exciting.

We took her through the game reserves, and showed her all of the big game roaming freely in their natural habitat. We were driving slowly up a small dirt trail in the middle of knee high grass. In the distance was a beautiful herd of gazelles. We stopped to watch them. They were so peacefully feeding, and enjoying their freedom. Suddenly to our right, a huge lion stood to his feet above the grass. He saw the deer also. He watched them, and we watched him. He moved quietly toward the herd. He would go a short distance, and then lie down – hidden by the grass. A few minutes later, he would get up, and continue to slowly and quietly move forward.

We sat still and watched. We wanted to see the climax, even though I hate to see a lion make a kill. The lion kept stalking – going closer and closer to the herd. He was almost upon them. Then suddenly they raised their heads, looked in the direction of the lion, and started running as quick as lighting. The lion simply watched them, but he didn't chase them. Instead, he came close to our vehicle, and crossed the little path in front of us. He stopped in the middle, and he looked at us with such a defeated and disgusted stare. *Hey, Mr. Lion, we didn't warn them, or cause them to run away from your dinner table.*

Mother was fascinated by the herds of zebra, elephants, giraffes, Cape buffaloes, and different species of deer. It is so much different to see these animals in their natural environment than in a zoo. They are born free and live free.

That Ostrich Was Hopping Mad

I think the experience which thrilled her most was when we happened upon an ostrich that was sitting on a nest of eggs. From a distance we saw the bird raise its long neck and head above the high grass. We knew that it was a male ostrich that was hatching eggs. Yes, the female lays them, but the male sits on the nest for weeks while they hatch.

We slowly drove over near to the nest. The huge bird jumped off the nest, and ran in front of the stopped car. He was visibly angry as he flapped his gigantic wings in front of the van. He was protecting the dozens of huge eggs that were in the nest. Getting out of the van to try to calm him down was not in our thoughts.

My mother was excited and scared. It was even my first time to see an angry, ten feet high ostrich so near us. He started to come to the side of the van, and Bill yelled at my mother, "Roll up the window! He will reach inside and peck the daylights out of you." She was so excited and scared she could hardly get the window rolled up. We laughed and laughed.

We watched for awhile as he flapped his wings, and warned us to leave. He even chased the van for a short distance. Did you know that an ostrich can run seventy miles an hour? Thankfully, he stopped quickly, and went back to hatching his babies. Mother talked about that experience until the Lord took her home.

A Trip to Mombasa

We also took Mother to the coast at Mombasa. It was approximately three hundred miles from Nairobi to Mombasa, and along the way she had the opportunity to see the giant ant hills that stand ten to twelve feet tall. They are quite a sight as they appear in the desert areas and look like small, red hills. They are really termites. When the rains come, they swarm from the hills. The Kenyans loved to catch them, pull off their wings, and eat them. They are a real delicacy – to the Kenyans – not to me!

They are enjoyed by various tribes, but particularly the Luhya tribe of Western Kenya. The termites are cooked, fried, or eaten raw. Sometimes they sprinkle a little salt on the live, raw termites and pop them in their mouths. Well, who likes meat without salt? They also make stew with them. I considered giving you a recipe for termite stew, but decided it would be a waste of my time and paper.

The termites are called "kumbi kumbi." They are different from the wood-eating termites in the States. They are rich in protein, and are a great snack – so I was told by my Kenyan friends. No, I never tried them. Even though I do love adventure - I also suffer from a weak stomach.

The Kenyan children would sometimes go into the fields during the rainy season with a basin. They would put the basin over the termites, catch them, and take them home. While their mom was preparing supper, they would wait until the glass chimney of the kerosene lamp was hot, then hold one termite by the wing, just above the glass for a few seconds, and then eat it. I was told termites have a sugary taste and a salty taste in the head region. Can't beat sweet and savory together!

The Kenyans know how to harvest them - for themselves or for commercial use. They would sometimes put a covering over the nest with only one hole in it. They would have a container set up next to the hole. Since the termites swarm when they hear the rain start, the Kenyans would trick them. They would put a long stick on the nest, or hill, then take two smaller sticks and drum on the long stick that was imbedded into the nest. They would drum as long as it took for the termites to think it was raining and they would swarm through the hole. Alas, they were caught and became a tasty meal.

Because of these flying termites, it was wise to keep the windows in the house closed during the rains. At night, they fly toward any light they see. My houseboy left my kitchen window open one day, and when I turned the light on at night, hundreds of them flew into the house. Of course, he was quite happy as he caught as many as possible for his supper.

Attacked by a Crocodile

During one of our outings, we visited a crocodile farm. We saw different ponds of water where the crocs were kept at different ages. As they grew, they were moved from one pond to another. We were there after dark, and it was a bit creepy to look out over those ponds in the dim light, and see only eyes above the water – staring at us.

One of the employees brought some eggs to us that were just ready to hatch. We could hear muffled sounds inside the eggs. He told me to hold one, and he cracked it open. A little baby croc about six inches long came wiggling out. He immediately launched onto my finger with his tiny, baby teeth. I could feel the pressure, but it didn't hurt. It just reassured me they are born killers!

Bill's Mother Went to Heaven

In October, during the time my mother was visiting with us, we received a call from Bill's sister in Ohio. His mother had been diagnosed with terminal cancer, and the doctor said she had six months to live. The family thought she didn't know about the diagnosis, and they were not telling her. She had cared for several family members before they died with cancer, and she feared she would die of it also.

"Bill, you should go home. I didn't make it home to see Dad, so you should go now."

"Well, if I show up there alone, she will be suspicious about why I am home by myself. We have to take your mother home anyway, so later we will just all go and tell her we have come home for Christmas. "

Two weeks later, he received another call - his mom was unresponsive and failing fast. He left the next day for the States. He arrived in the night, and planned to go to the hospital the next morning - but she died that night. We had prayed she wouldn't suffer, and God answered our prayers. It hurts to be so far away from loved ones when God takes them home. Bill's dad died while we were in Australia, but we didn't have the money for him to go for the funeral – just one other sacrifice we missionaries must make in order to follow the call of God upon our lives.

Shaleen was still in Nairobi when Wyvonna and Greg came for Christmas. It was wonderful to have Christmas with all three of our children and my mother that year.

We booked a Pan Am flight for the kids and Mother to return to the States in January. During that time, classified information came into KUSLO that the terrorists had threatened to place a bomb on a Pan Am flight to the States during the Christmas holiday season. We were always having threats, and we learned never to take all of them seriously. The terrorists want to keep people in a state of fear. The threats were never overlooked, but at the same time people had to continue their normal life - unless there was specific information that made the threat credible. Usually if there is going to be an attack, they don't warn people about it.

We debated as to whether we should postpone the flight. The threat had not targeted the plane they would be flying on. It was important for Greg to get back to college, and for Wyvonna and Shaleen to go back to work. God spoke to our hearts and assured us that they would be okay. We decided to trust Him, and let them continue on the flight. It was difficult to say goodbye to our three kids and my mother at the airport that day. We would miss them so much. We prayed for their safety, and God delivered them home without harm. In December 1988, the terrorists did put a bomb on Pan Am Flight 103 which exploded over Lockerbie, Scotland and killed 259 people.

Chapter 30
A Painful Experience

I was getting ready for bed when I started itching. *A* hive? No, hundreds of them were appearing all over my body. I tried not to scratch, but after a while, scratching is pure delight – temporarily. Then my head started to itch! Oh, yes, I was having a major reaction to something - but what? I had not eaten anything different. To my knowledge, I had not been bitten by anything. Oh no, they moved to my mouth. As the huge, red hives started down my throat, Bill and I started to the hospital about twenty minutes from our home.

By the time we got there, I was not only itching – I was hurting! We went to the Emergency Room and to the front desk. By then I was really in pain. I was told to take a seat and wait. Some things are the same as in America.

I tried to be patient in my pain, realizing that others were also in pain, and needed to see doctors. A doctor finally checked me, and asked me a hundred questions about what I had eaten. *No - no shellfish. No, I had not been at the coast. No, nothing had bitten me. No, no, no, no.* He did not know what was causing the condition, but he said it could be serious, so he was going to admit me to the hospital. Thank you!

Then I waited – and waited – and waited! My joints were hurting so badly I was almost in tears. I have never had joint pain like that before.

A Painful Experience

I kept asking, "When am I going to a room? I need to lie down?"

"We are waiting for someone to take you to your room."

I continued to wait while every joint in my body hurt, especially my knees. I tried to keep calm in my pain, and act like a Christian. However, after about two hours, my patience exploded.

"When can I go to my room?" I asked the nurse. Sometimes it is so hard to maintain a sweet, Christian attitude. At that time, they did not know I was a missionary – but God knew. Don't you just wish you could hide sometimes and explode without harming your testimony before God and people?

"Be patient. We are waiting for someone to come and take you to the room."

By now, the pain was ruining my attitude, and my patience was already gone.

"I know the hospital. Just tell me what room number I am going to, and I will go there by myself." By then I was really praying – for enough self-control to keep from trying to hurt someone!

The nurse finally told me what room I was going to be in, and I said to Bill, "Come on. I've got to lie down."

I started down the hall, and each step was a struggle. My only comfort was in knowing if I could take a few more steps, I could collapse into a bed - if I could force my aching knees to cooperate.

When I finally made it to the room, I fell into bed in my clothes. A nurse suggested I change into a hospital gown. Not a good suggestion at that moment! She was a quick learner. Soon someone came and gave me a shot. The rest of the night is dim in my memory. I think I slept in my clothes.

I was still hurting in all of my joints the next day, even though the hives were disappearing. At least I was seeing some action on the part of the medical staff. They were running numerous blood tests, and giving me medication while they were trying to determine what had caused the reaction.

Later in the day, several people from the medical staff visited my room. First, a pleasant British man popped in, and introduced himself as the Hospital Administrator. He asked me questions about my experience in the ER the night before. I spewed out all the details, and he apologized profusely. He was so friendly, and wanted to know what he could do for me.

"What can I do to make you more comfortable? What would you like? What about a lobster and steak dinner? Just speak the word and it's yours."

"Thank you, but all I want is for you to quickly cure me, and get me out of here."

"You just let me know if there is anything you want."

Just after he left, others started to visit me – including the head nurse and the staff who were on duty in the ER the night before. They all apologized to me! Hmmmm. I wonder why? Could it be my condition could have brought about my death? And maybe they would have been responsible? I did have to wait for three hours to get treatment for such a horrific allergic reaction.

I had great attention and treatment for the next three days, but I still felt so badly I couldn't enjoy it. I left the hospital without ever knowing what had caused my near death experience. I thank God He was taking care of me.

I was thankful I was in the Nairobi Hospital instead of the Jomo Kenyatta Hospital - the government hospital where most of the Kenyans went for free treatment. I would not have been treated so well there. In fact, I don't think I would ever have gone to the hospital if that was my only choice.

Mary Was Near Death

One night Mary sent one of her children to our house. "Come quickly. My mama is sick."

We went to Mary's little house in the back yard. She was so sick and so pale, she almost looked white. We quickly put her in the car, and took her to the Jomo Kenyatta Hospital.

On the way, she told me she had seen a vision of her little girl who had died when she was about four years old.

Mary said, "I saw her. She was standing with her arms stretched toward me, saying 'Come on, mama.' I know she is in Heaven, and she was trying to get me to come to her."

I really believe Mary was near death, and maybe she did see her daughter. I can't explain it, but I have heard many stories like Mary's. I know just before one of our missionaries (Michelle Stringfield) died; she said she saw her mother and her grandmother just before she took her last breath. They were both in Heaven.

Mary was admitted to the hospital, and stayed for about a week. The first time we went to visit her; I was appalled at the conditions. We were directed to a large ward. We went inside a long room. Beds were on both sides of the room. There were only about four feet between the beds. But the most surprising thing was that there were two women in each bed – one at the head of the bed and one at the foot. These were single hospital beds. Two women were under the beds on mattresses!! There were no sheets or pillow cases on any of the beds. It was appalling!

We walked down the long room to Mary's bed. I almost had to hold my breath, because the odor was so strong in the ward. They had an IV in Mary's arm. I looked at the floor under the pole, and saw blood sprinkled there.

We went out to the nurse's station to talk to them. On the counter was a used needle with blood under it. I don't know how anyone lived through the hospital experience, but Mary survived. TIK.

Chapter 31
Challenges for a Missionary

Many people over the years have asked me, "What is the greatest difficulty a missionary faces?" Most missionaries face many of the same challenges, but I will not speak for others – just for myself.

I was raised in a non-Christian family, and I had attended church about six times in my life. Oh, yes, I know the number, because I remember each time and place when I went to church. About two months before I graduated from high school, I attended a revival meeting at the Burton Baptist Church in Flint, Michigan. That night I heard the gospel. I already realized I was going to Hell, but I heard that Jesus died to keep me from going there. Pastor Edmund Dinant counseled with me for two hours after church, and I asked Jesus to forgive me for my sins. I was saved!

Three months later, I surrendered my life totally to the Lord. I told Him I would go anywhere, and do anything he wanted me to do. Soon after that commitment, I felt God was leading me to the Baptist Bible College in Springfield, Missouri to prepare for his will for my life – whatever it was. I obeyed God, and in doing so, I totally disobeyed my unsaved parents. That was difficult, and a great challenge for me early in my Christian life.

When I surrendered my life to God, this little Arkansas girl had no idea God might want me to be a missionary! During my second year in college, I felt God was calling me to the mission field. Not just the mission field - but Africa! This surrender of my will took a few days longer than the first time. But, finally I told God, *I don't want to be a missionary. I don't think I have what it takes to be a missionary. But, Lord, if that's what you want me to do; I am willing, if you will give me the strength and grace to do it.*

In my last year of college, I made another commitment. I promised my husband, Bill Cunningham, that I would marry him and live with him "until death do us part."

When we first went to the mission field of Ethiopia, I was twenty-four years old. I had been saved only five years. We had two daughters; Wyvonna was almost two years old, Shaleen was seven months old, and I was three months pregnant with our son, Greg. Crazy? Well, we are fools for Christ's sake. *Yes, it was a challenge. It was also difficult to leave my unsaved family, my country, and all that was familiar to me.*

The next challenge came soon after our arrival in Ethiopia - when we started to language school. Amharic was not an easy language. Well, no new language is easy, but Amharic is one of the harder ones to learn. In my pregnant condition, I waddled to classes five days a week. It was not easy to leave our babies with an Ethiopian nanny. *That was a challenge.*

It was also a challenge to give birth to our son in a crude, mission hospital with an American Adventist doctor who, because of their religious belief, refused to put me to sleep in an extremely difficult delivery. It was so difficult that I went into shock after Greg was born. It took quick and continued action for the doctors and nurses to stabilize me. Yes, *that was difficult.*

The new culture is always a difficult adjustment for missionaries. I could write a book on culture shock. It can be so overwhelming at times. A woman has to learn how to shop, and cook in the new country. The language barrier continues to be a problem for a long time. Raising children in a third world country is a huge challenge. A missionary must always be careful about cleanliness to prevent sickness.

Loneliness is another great challenge – especially on holidays. We missed the family during Thanksgiving and Christmas. We knew they would be celebrating together while we were thousands of miles away.

It is scary when war comes to your mission field, as it did in Ethiopia, and the missionary family must leave the country. You can read all about this in my first book, "Oh Lord, What Have I Gotten Myself Into?" We went to Ethiopia with the intention of remaining there the rest of our lives, but we had to move on. We went from Ethiopia to Australia (without returning to America). Let me insert another commercial at this point. I think you would find my second book about Australia interesting – "Glad I Didn't Know."

Missionaries face all kinds of sickness on the mission field, and many times the medical help and facilities are not adequate. Children's schooling is another large difficulty in a foreign country. There are usually only two options – boarding school or home school. Neither of them is ideal.

Oh, yes, these are only a few of the challenges most missionaries cope with for years. One of the greatest challenges for me was to leave our three teenage children in the States after they graduated from high school. Missionary children have not been raised in the United States, so America is really not their home. They suffer their own culture shock when they usually have to stay in America without their parents. To them, America is a big, scary, foreign country. It broke my heart when we had to leave our children in America, and go back to the mission field.

The kids struggled. Greg continued in college. Wyvonna and Shaleen worked and tried to fit into American culture. They had a hard time. They felt different. Their lives had evolved around traveling, living in foreign countries, and boarding school. Their peers had lived only in America, and their lives were filled with sports, American churches, and normal teen activities. They didn't have a lot in common. Missionary kids feel like foreigners when they return to America - because they are Americans by citizenship only. People don't understand why they don't fit in immediately.

Shaleen married a few months after she returned from Kenya. She had a basic need to be loved and to have a home. However, she didn't live happily ever after. Her husband was not the man she thought him to be. She suffered in the marriage, but she didn't want to worry us, so she never told us what was happening. After our grandson, Shane, was born, we learned she was in trouble.

I have faced many challenges over the years, but *my greatest challenge and heartache was when I learned Shaleen was in an abusive marriage*, and I was thousands of miles away from her and our infant grandson. She was in immediate danger. What would you have done? What would be your reactions?

We had not changed our minds about serving the Lord, but God told us if we don't provide for our household we are worse than an infidel. Does he refer just to food, clothing, and shelter while they are children? Do they ever cease to be your children? We could not stand by and watch our daughter and grandson being abused.

Sometimes, as in our case, God permits a delay in route. We made the decision our daughter needed us, so we left Kenya and came back to America. We rescued her and our grandson from a frightening situation. It took some time to establish her and Wyvonna. Greg graduated from college, got a good job, and was quite independent. He is now an executive with Graybar Electric Corporation in St. Louis, Missouri, and is married and has two little boys, Hunter and Carter. Wyvonna married a career soldier, who is now retired from the Army, and is doing civilian contracting with the military. She has a son, Phillip, and is a stay-at-home mom. Shaleen remarried, went back to college after forty years old, and graduated with honors. She now works as a paralegal with a law firm. Her son, Shane, is a proud United States Marine, and her daughter, Veronika, is a senior in high school.

When the time was right, we again returned to the mission field. Our commitment to God was not finished. It will not be finished until He calls us home. We have labored in various countries – because of circumstances, not our choosing. But, we have never come to the point where we said, *Okay, Lord, we have fought a good fight, we have finished our course.* Paul made that statement just before going to Heaven. We plan to keep following God's course for us (missions) and fighting the battles until we draw our last breath in death, or until we hear the trumpet sound, and hear a voice saying, "Come up hither." Until that day, and Lord willing, I will continue to write the rest of our story.

Chapter 32
Memories from my Daughter, Shaleen

I don't remember the trips to the airports and the gut wrenching goodbyes. My mind tends to block out traumatic experiences. It's amazing how we are programmed in different ways for self preservation and survival instincts. Mine is mental blocks. My mind locks things away. A scary thought is if that mental vault ever opens!! Stand back!!

On the other hand, I was not leaving people I knew. I was never around them long enough to create a bond that was painfully broken each time we left. Some missionary kids build a wall to getting close to anyone to avoid these painful separations. Some try too hard to fit in, to try to make a place for themselves then end up being hurt, resulting in the wall of avoidance. It is a major insecurity to not know where you belong or to not know where your roots are, and where you tie into them. This might also be part of the reason I don't remember the goodbyes.

I really enjoyed traveling, and I still do. When I was younger, and we traveled through different countries on our way to our final destination, I usually had uneasiness about something happening to Mom and Dad. Where would I go? What would I do? I didn't have a home, and didn't know my relatives. I was the sensitive child, so these thoughts usually haunted me.

Memories from my Daughter, Shaleen

I am a visual learner, so visiting different countries made history come alive for me when we actually saw places that were written about in history books! I have to say, though, my American History is still lacking, and I constantly learn new things - even after being in America for many years. Fortunately, my husband is a bit of a history buff and helps me along. He kindly overlooks my odd statements about politics and my confusion about the North versus the South, etc. I am actually still learning things about America that come up occasionally in conversation or television. My teenage daughter really soaks up history, so she teaches me a lot too.

When I first came back to America to live, I was almost nineteen years old. You have to understand that I started school in Australia, and at that time the Australians were a bit anti-American, so we never learned anything about America growing up in the Australian school system. As I got older, whatever I heard in higher grades didn't really penetrate since I did not live in America. So I had a few incidents which I can laugh at now… well, I laughed at them then actually!

I went to work in an office in Jacksonville, Florida and the girl who was suppose to show me around was telling me about her, and seemed very impressed with the fact that she had worked at a place called "Pentagon." I said, "Oh, that's nice." She repeated about three times this "Pentagon" place where she seemed so proud to have worked, but I basically let her know I was happy for her and wanted to know what my responsibilities were in the office. After work that day I went home and called Mom in Africa to tell her how my first day went. I told her about this girl, and the fact that she seemed to be so proud to have worked at some building that started with a "P." Mom asked, "The Pentagon?" I said, "Oh, yes, you've heard of it?"

The adjustment to America could be a whole book! I now know what the Pentagon is and why the North was against the

South even though it's called "United States" and that I am a rebel! I also realize, after quite a shock, that different states have different accents!

My first memory of Kenya is going into town in Nairobi with two other missionary kids, Jon Konnerup and Jay Piercy. We rode a city bus, and an African woman sitting next to me started feeding her baby...au natural! I tried to focus on something else, and found a sign at the front of the bus – "Usivute Sigara." I will never forget those words! I read them over and over until we got off the bus and then asked Jon and Jay what it meant. They told me it meant, "No Smoking." It's not a Swahili statement I can use much, but it certainly helped me in a time of need! When we got back to our parents after our excursion, one of the missionary ladies asked me if I was surprised by all the white faces I saw. I guess "Usivute Sigara" could have come in useful then, because I figured she must have been smoking some strange African weed!

I don't remember the long ride to our boarding school - Rift Valley Academy (RVA). Remember, sensitive child, plus traumatic experience, equals mental lockdown! I do remember my first sight of our dorm. It was made with grey cinder blocks and all the windows had bars on them! Mental lockdown! We are now entering prison!! We were told it was to keep people out for our safety. Right! Some of the students seemed to deal well with their emotional collapse as they ran around with butterfly nets like lunatics - at least that's how my sister explained it as I was still in mental lockdown. Little did I know that I would soon succumb to the lunacy myself, as it was required by our Biology teacher. My sister never weakened to the constraints of the academic pressure. She was happy to take an "F" in the class. She once described me as a follower. I guess I was, because I believe I made an "A" on my board of pinned butterflies.

After my parents helped us unload our luggage and settled us into our dorm rooms, we said our goodbyes. As I watched them drive off, I felt like I was hit in the chest with a baseball. (I know how this feels because I actually took a line drive to the chest once.) After my parents left, I held myself together since I was not one of those poor little first graders who had every reason to cry when their parents left them there. But once inside the privacy of my dorm room, I released the pressure from my eyes and the large lump in my throat that had been trying to explode all day. I was glad that my sister and I were able to room together, although, she was not quite sensitive to my plight. She and I express ourselves differently. I over-analyze, whereas she jumps right in.

Rift Valley Academy used the British system for schooling. Therefore, we went to school year-round - three months in, one month out. My brother, sister and I were fortunate enough to be able to go home for the one month breaks, but most of the other kids' parents lived farther away so the students lived on campus throughout the year. When classes started, I was given a list of all the assignments and reports I would have completed by the end of the year. This put me bawling on my sister's shoulder and wanting to go home! Years later I still look back at that and remind myself, "One day at a time. One obstacle at a time." In fact, "one day at a time" has been my New Year's resolution for the past five or six years.

I finally got in the groove of my new life in the middle of Africa - way up on a mountain in the middle of nothing but three large volcanoes! The largest one was named Longanot, and it was active. That did not keep the school from scheduling camping trips on, and in, Longanot. I never had the great fortune to experience that. I fell into a volcano in New Zealand once, but it was inactive, so it's not as exciting a story as camping in an active one! Maybe one day I can do that. I will put it on my Bucket List!

One night while everyone was furiously studying for end-of-term exams, I was walking back to my dorm from the library. Longanot was in view as I walked out of the library door onto the outside porch of Kiambogo. Kiambogo was the main building in the middle of the school. The word, "Kiambogo" is Swahili for "Place where the buffalo roam." I saw smoke and red fire light coming out of Longonot! I ran to the dorm announcing that Longanot was erupting!! If Longanot erupted, we were close enough to be engulfed in hot smoldering lava!! This is what I had been told anyway. Everyone ran out of the dorms to watch the last moments of our lives as we knew them, when the dorm parents yelled for everyone to return to the dorms and back to their studying, because Longonot was just having one of its many fires! Longanot has a forest inside it with wild animals that live there. I guess it hasn't erupted in quite a while, but it certainly makes an exciting story! And I was not the only one who believed we faced our deaths that night!

My body finally adjusted to the altitude after three months! I was able to walk across campus or up stairs without almost passing out. A change in altitude changes the functioning of your body! I now understand why recipes have different instructions for higher altitudes. Things don't work like they should. I also understand why Kenyans win a lot of sporting events when they are in America. They are at a big advantage with the lower altitude and thinner air. They can breathe better and run faster. Their bodies feel lighter.

We had to play rugby for P.E. I am not athletically inclined! Also being new, I was not familiar with rugby. I quickly learned how to "huddle." A "huddle" is when everyone grabs you, and this group is surrounding the ball, trying to maneuver it to their goal. Trust me - you don't want your head and body sticking up above the huddle while it is forcing you forward, backward, and side to side! It's called a "scrum," and this is how the internet explained it on "Rugby Sidestep Central":

"Eight players from each team bind together in their own 3-4-1 formation in a crouching position. The two formations engage each other head on to form a single mass of 16 players. The ball is then put into the tunnel between the opposing formations and each team attempts to get control of the ball with their feet."

Before a scrum is formed, there is a "maul." Here is the explanation of a maul:

"Using the skill and qualities of the forwards, the maul is a technique for keeping control of the ball and moving the ball towards (and sometimes into) the opposition in-goal area. The ball can be moved from player to player within the maul as long as the maul keeps moving towards one of the goal lines and the players stay bound together. The maul is like a small swarm of bees with the ball tucked inside. Coordinate the pushing, vary the direction, smuggle the ball between players, move the ball forward. **Stay Bound!** If the ball is trapped within a maul that is not moving, a scrum will be set and the team not in possession of the ball will get the advantage of putting the ball into the scrum."

So there you have it. That was not a good mix for someone who is not athletic, even though I wanted to play sports. I tried out for field hockey. I didn't make it. I still wonder if it was my lack of athletic ability or the fact that I accidently mistook one of the other player's hand for the puck. She healed quickly without need for stitches and made the team. I decided it was safer for me to attend sporting events for the social aspect.

Classes went well as far as I can remember…mental block. One problem with living at school is everyone knows everyone too well, teachers included. Personalities mesh or clash. Mine clashed with my Swahili teacher. Or maybe he was just a mean person. Imagine never being able to get far from your students! Most of the dorm parents were teachers, so we were around each other constantly! I didn't need Swahili anyway. Everyone spoke English, and the Africans wanted to learn better English, so they wouldn't speak Swahili to us.

On school days "chai time" was mid-morning. Chai is Swahili for tea. Don't get it confused with Choo (Cho) which means toilet. We would all line up with our mugs to get chai, and if we had coffee cake for breakfast that morning, we would get whatever was left over - and even the next day if there was still some left over. The coffee cake wasn't too bad, but once we had chocolate cake for dessert and someone threw it at the window – I don't know why – but it broke the window and stayed in one piece on the other side!

We had metal, army type trays to eat from in the cafeteria. The menu consisted of a variety of foods including British dishes, Indian dishes, American dishes, etc. It was pretty good... except the time I found a roach hiding under my baked chicken. I don't think he had been baked with it, I think he decided to start lunch without me! We had visitors like that every now and then. Once it was a rat running around our feet. Another time a bat was swooping over our heads.

Mealtimes were not usually boring. Although, I guess we did get bored with no visitors one day, so I started a food fight... yep...I earned a weekend of enjoying my own company in my dorm room.

The last year I was there the school put in a salad bar! We felt really special and that kept us amused for a while. Sometimes we had pancakes for breakfast. The pancakes were pretty good, but we had to make sure the servers put the syrup on the pancakes, because it was literally the consistency of water! If it was put in one of the compartments on the tray, there would be none left by the time we got to our seat. It would be on the floor and on us!

If we were lucky enough to have bread (white only) at a meal, a lot of the kids would collect unwanted slices and take a fist-full of them back to the dorm and toast them on the heat register or iron for a late night snack.

Another snack that seemed to be a delicacy was acquired after a hard rain. If a window was left open, "flying ants" - which were really large termites - would fly in swarms into the room. I think the girls in the dorm left the window open on purpose since they were really excited to scoop up a bowl full of the termites. One of the girls showed me the proper way to eat a raw one! She held the wings and said, "You give one bite and swallow, and then throw the wings away." I guess the wings are not edible. The favorite thing to do was to pull the wings off and fry a bunch of them in butter and salt. The result was small black lumps with little legs sticking up. I mustered some courage and tried one, but quickly spit it out since the thought of it just grossed me out. I was not brave enough to put a live one in my mouth - or did it have nothing to do with bravery?

The cafeteria line was long for most meals, so you wanted to get there early except on baked fish day - if it was actually baked fish! The smell was horrible! On "baked fish" day the line was very short on campus, but very long down the hill at the Duka. The Duka was the African "café." It was a small wooden shack probably 20' x 15'. The kitchen consisted of a fire built on the dirt floor. I don't even want to know how they stored food items! I remember an old beat up wooden "counter" where we ordered our food. There was only one table inside where the Africans usually sat. If we were early enough, we could sit inside with them. My favorite food to order was either egg-on-toast or a mandazi. I usually got the mandazi which was square, sweet bread that tasted like a donut. The egg-on-toast was made like French toast, but the bread was freshly made – somewhere – and it was about an inch thick. It was flavorful enough without syrup. I don't want to know why. Somehow we never got sick!

If we ever got sick or hurt, we went to the infirmary, or sometimes we would go and just say we were sick or hurt, like when President Daniel Arap Moi came to speak at chapel. We knew he would speak for at least two hours! So a couple of us decided to go to the infirmary for an excuse to miss chapel, and the nurse would make us the best cinnamon toast!! I learned that eating chalk or shaking the thermometer upside down raised your temperature. We didn't have the fancy digital ones there, or maybe the right word is "then." We are talking about a "few" years back. So, yes, we missionary kids told little white lies from time to time! I believe I actually might have learned some of these sinful habits in America.

On one of our furloughs, Dad traveled while Mom and we kids lived in an apartment so we could go to school. I think I was in the sixth grade. I was outside and saw a group of girls. They called me over to talk to me and asked if I wanted to play "hooky" tomorrow. I was very excited that I might have found some friends - and they seemed to like me! I quickly replied, "Sure! How do you play?" Needless to say, I did not get to play hooky the next day, and those girls found my naivety more amusing to them than playing hooky. The rest of my time in that school was quite disturbing, and I learned more than the three R's!

I've never been one to cause very much trouble - at least I didn't see it as causing trouble. I think it is what teenagers call "expressing themselves." There were limited activities at RVA, so it could be boring at times. The main on-going activity at night was the Student Center. Most of us would go there after dinner - that's where the chocolate cake was thrown through the window. Everyone sat around and talked while listening to music which was mostly ABBA, since the censoring was so strict. Maybe ABBA had subliminal messaging which caused someone to throw the cake through the window, or maybe they just got tired of hearing Dancing Queen over and over again.

We used to have a fuse ball table until we demolished it with our aggressive competitiveness. Fuse ball was one sport in which I became quite accomplished.

With the fuse ball table gone, there was a large open space, so we started a new game called Red Rover. It was quickly banned after a few injuries and destruction of property. I believe it was at this point there was nothing left to do except plan other exciting forms of entertainment. Since we lived together - let me clarify that, boys dorms were down the hill and girls dorms were up the hill - what could be new to talk about that we didn't already know? If we were caught sneaking out after curfew or off campus without permission, the punishment of choice was being campused which meant we could go to classes and meals then back to our room. I learned to enjoy the solitude of my room. Some friends came up from Nairobi on their motorcycles, so a friend and I went off campus with them for a ride down the mountain then back up - but we went without permission and got caught. After a two-week campusing, (for going off campus without permission), my friends and I had a party to celebrate freedom.

We had to be careful if we sneaked out of the dorm at night, because there were "askaris" (guards) who walked the grounds "protecting" us, so if they saw someone on the grounds, they usually shot their arrows before asking any questions. It was very important to announce yourself and state your business before this happened.

We had a laundry room where we sent our clothes to be washed. The girls had lingerie bags for their "delicates." I accidently received someone else's lingerie bag. This person shall remain nameless. I tied her delicates together to form a rope. I was going to string this "delicate rope" from one basketball hoop to the other on the basketball court - which was positioned in full view of Kiambogo. I sneaked out the back fire escape - after curfew - with the bag stuffed in my coat. I got to the bottom of the steps when an askari popped around from the side of the building. Those guys wore long black coats and black hats with face masks, so it was quite a shock when you saw them. Also, they were very quiet. At night it was so dark you couldn't even see your hand in front of you! So it was easy to run right into them and scare them as bad as they scared us! I told him, "Jambo" (hello), then turned and ran back up the steps. So all I was able to do was send the lingerie bag back to the laundry. But, at least it was funny because when she pulled one out, they all came out like one of those clowns' hankies! Yes, I am easily amused!

Some things we didn't want to send to the laundry if we wanted them to come back in one piece. We preferred to wash our jeans in our dorm laundry room which had two large sinks. We hand-washed the jeans with OMO washing soap then grabbed whoever was walking by to help twist all the water out before hanging them to dry.

We were assigned dorm jobs which changed every week. Nobody liked the job of scrubbing the old wax off the hall floors with steel wool, then mopping them good and re-waxing them. But the worst job was to stoke the fire at night. We had to keep the fire going or we did not have hot water in the dorm. As I said earlier, it was so dark outside, and I was afraid of the dark. I never wanted to go alone. Buffalo were known to still roam the area. There were also rumors of a 3-legged leopard and one of the most poisonous snakes - the black mamba - lived around there! (One of our teachers had been bitten by a snake when she was younger and had to have her arm cut off!) And if none of those horrors got you, there was always an askari hiding around the corner! And we *were* in the middle of Africa, so there was no telling what else was out there!

One night I went to stoke the fire, and my friend went with me. She waited around the corner for me after I collected some wood from the pile.

Memories from my Daughter, Shaleen

I entered the small tin shack which was attached to the end of the dorm, and it was surrounded by the African woods. The wind blew branches against the tin roof above me. The ground was slightly damp from the rain earlier in the day. The only light I had to guide me was the glow of the flames that were visible around the edges of the furnace door. The only comfort I felt was in knowing that my friend was around the corner to run for help if I was suddenly attacked by something or somebody.

I slowly lowered myself to the level of the furnace door. I held the wood in one hand as I reached for the furnace door handle with the other hand. I felt uneasy. The wind whistled, the branches screeched on the tin. In the dampness I felt a presence. My heart began to race! Suddenly, a bright light shone from above - right into my face! I fell back paralyzed! I heard the male voice say, "Jambo." The askari was sitting cross-legged on the concrete casing above the furnace, and decided to announce himself at my most vulnerable moment!! I dropped the wood and ran! I guess the Askari was kind enough to put the wood in the furnace, because we had hot water the next morning. I was appreciative, because the work chart was posted on the wall so everyone knew who was responsible.

Another night we didn't have hot water because as I walked around the corner to the tin shack, I saw someone in the shack! I turned and tried to run, but I couldn't get traction on the damp ground. My feet ran in place for a few seconds before I could make my final departure! Later I found out that the two in the shack were students who were making out!

My brother said one of the African cafeteria workers he knew was walking through those African woods to work one morning when he was attacked by a buffalo. It gored him through the leg and ran with him. The man tried to punch the buffalo in the eye, but was hanging low around his neck with the buffalo's horn in his leg. He couldn't reach the eye so the only thing he could do was squeeze his nostril as hard as he could. The buffalo didn't like that and threw him off. The man was able to get to the school to get help. He required many stitches, but survived.

Although the wildlife of Africa can be frightening, it can also be the object of pranks and just general fun. One of my classmates had a six foot boa constrictor as a pet. I'm not sure how he angled permission to keep it in his dorm room. I'm also not sure how he continued to have permission to keep the boa after a prank he pulled in Psychology class!

He sneaked into class with the snake before everyone else arrived, and put it in one of the desks. The desk was the old type which had the hinged lid. Approximately ten or fifteen minutes after class began, the girl, who was unfortunate enough to be sitting in that desk, lifted the desk top to get something. She did not expect to get a six foot boa staring up at her! She screamed, we laughed, and the class was quickly dismissed since any semblance of order after that was impossible!

I liked the boa. He seemed harmless enough. He was smooth and cool to the touch. I liked to play with him and let him slither around my waist. He liked to go inside my shirt, wrap around my waist and pop his head up through the neck hole. He never squeezed too tightly, but when it seemed like he was getting a little too comfortable, we would unwrap him and let him have some alone time in his cage. I kissed him on the mouth to say goodbye, and he flickered his tongue at me contently. So, I can actually say I've kissed a snake in my lifetime!

Sometimes we had to deal with bats. They lived in the Mau Mau caves around the school. The caves ran under the school and were used by the Mau Mau to hide when they planned their attack on our school in the 1950's. Sometimes we liked to explore the caves, but didn't spend a lot of time in them since the inside was lined with bats. Now and then a bat would find its way to our dorm. One such time, was in our "dating parlor." He was flopping around on the floor, so I grabbed a bucket and put over him. We then slid a piece of cardboard under the bucket to enclose the bat. We took him outside and released him. One time as Mom and Dad traveled up the mountain to visit us, a bat hit the windshield and stuck to the wiper blade. It was dangerous to stop anywhere coming up that mountain because there were thieves and thugs, so Mom and Dad had to wait until they arrived at the school before they could let the bat loose. TIK.

Another cave which was interesting was in "Hell's Gate." We went there for a field trip before it was a national park. Hell's Gate was located near the volcano, Longanot. It was named Hell's Gate because of the hot steam geysers that shot up out of the ground. Cool molten lava from volcanoes formed obsidian, which is a black, glass-like rock. We had to chip off a piece of the obsidian and chisel an arrow out of it like Neanderthals! We had to be very careful, because that glass-like rock would chip into thin, sharp shards that cut like the worst paper cut you ever had! It was interesting, and I certainly preferred being outdoors rather than cooped up in the classroom.

Although I like being outdoors, I do have my limits - and limitations. One of our learning experiences was called "Interim." We were required to fill out a form with three selections of what we would prefer to do during this educational trip called "Interim." Some of the more fortunate were lucky enough to go to Mombasa. I was late in choosing (I don't remember why), so I ended up on bike safari. One would think in taking a group of kids on a trip like that, it would not seem unreasonable to have forms or questionnaires for parents to fill out and sign. There were no forms. There were no medical histories, or even legal documentation saying, "No, we will not sue you if our child is eaten by a lion." I was never asked if I was physically fit with no allergies, etc. I didn't know the last time I rode a 10-speed bike…or if I ever did! But that didn't seem to concern them. I was more than a little confused on how to work all those gears!! I was not prepared physically or mentally for a 3-day ride on a 10-speed bike across the African wilderness! We were going to be gone for a week so I thought we were going to bike to the destination and bike back. To my great pleasure, I learned after the first day of riding, that we would be taking a bus back to the school!

After the first day of riding approximately seven or eight hours in the hot sun and wilderness of Africa, I felt like I had given birth to a rhino!! It was a good thing we had to ride the next day because I certainly couldn't walk! I guess the next two days went better since my whole bottom half was paralyzed by the pain of being impaled by a small bike seat, while baking to a medium rare in what felt like King Nebuchadnezzar's furnace! They did make sure throughout the trip that we took salt pills. I wouldn't want a lion to have to suffer through dry meat if I was dehydrated!

Our mental state was already fried or we wouldn't have been on a 3-day bike trek across the equator! Since I was not in shape for that trip, I was always the one lagging behind. Somehow that didn't seem to concern the teacher who was leading the group. I remember being alone for what seemed like hours and looking around seeing nothing but dry sand, bushes and a view that went on for miles. I wondered what two-legged or four-legged savages lurked in the bushes waiting for the kill! I pedaled faster! I know my guardian angels were with me. Even though it seemed like I was alone for so many hours, they gave me peace… even when I rode through the swarm of African Killer bees. Not one sting! "O death where is your sting…?"

This was supposed to be an educational trip. I don't remember learning anything except how to not panic and how to stay alive! I guess it has come in handy here in America. I did see the gorgeous pink flamingos at Lake Nakuru! They were sure more attractive than the plastic ones people put in their yards around here!

We traveled to Mombasa by train for our senior trip. It was called "Senior Safari." Everything is a safari over there. We vacationed in style. Africa isn't all grass huts and hippo poo! They have gorgeous 5-star resorts there. We stayed at the Two Fishes Hotel on Diani Beach. I don't know what it looks like now, but it was really nice back then. We enjoyed the beach and the nice pools. I was sitting in the shallow pool cooling off when I felt something jump on my head. All of a sudden whatever was on my head dove into the pool in front of me, then quickly shimmied up my arm to my shoulder and jumped again! It was a little monkey who must have thought I was a new addition to the pool! He jumped off my head and shoulders about 4 or 5 times! I didn't want to disturb him - since he was having so much fun! Also, because earlier that day my friend and I were talking to a lady when a monkey reached in the lady's purse and took her cigarettes out. I directed her attention to the monkey. He saw me do that and jumped up and bit me on the arm! He left the cutest little miniature teeth prints on my arm! Thankfully he didn't bring blood but I still like to tease that I have monkey blood!

Graduation finally arrived and I don't remember a thing about it! No, I'm just kidding, kind of. The source of my mental lockdown was the realization of flying back to America a few days later. Mom had a catalog from America, and she let my sister and me choose a dress that we could wear at graduation. My favorite color is purple, so I was happy to find a purple one. I do remember we were a graduating class of 98; the largest class to graduate. Also, we were the very first class to have caps and gowns! My sister and I pushed to make that happen, and we succeeded!

I have a few RVA friends on Facebook, so I asked them if they remember much about graduation since I do not. One of my old roommates told me she wasn't surprised I didn't remember, since we were all sick that week! A lot of us went to the infirmary – probably didn't feel like eating the cinnamon toast – and the rest of us were sick in our beds. Maybe we had some sort of African fever. I know I made it to the ceremony, because I remember just wanting the talking to be over and to get on with it! Somebody even sang a special - I think! Oh, come on!

Oh, I remember cake! Mom made a really nice cake with an airplane flying around the world. It was very tasty, but the fact that I had to fly to the other side of the world to start my new life put a very bad taste in my mouth! My sister and I tried to pack, but we kept fighting with each other. The heat rose with our anxiety and fear, so that was our outlet. Finally Dad called a meeting and we all discovered we were not ready to leave Africa and go to this place called "home."

For our graduation trip, my parents took my sister and me to Amboseli Game Reserve. We camped in a mud hut that had a cook stove of some sort, but I don't remember about indoor plumbing…I guess my self preservation mental block went into effect. Maybe I don't want to remember. We enjoyed the monkeys outside. They were climbing up my leg and digging in my pockets for a treat. Dad gave me some peanuts, and I put them in my pockets so the monkeys would have a successful dig.

I have some sort of magnetism when it comes to monkeys. It started when I was about four years old when we were on our way to the hippo pool. I had a fist full of cookies in one hand, and the other hand held the cookie I was eating. Suddenly a monkey ran up one of my legs, up over my head and grabbed the cookie I was eating out of my hand and ran into the bushes! I was hysterical! Dad told me to throw the other cookies down. I threw them down and monkeys came out of the bushes everywhere and stole all my cookies!! Surprisingly, I am not

Memories from my Daughter, Shaleen

terrified of monkeys. I actually love them! Now, big dogs, that's another story!

Amboseli was very interesting and we saw a lot of animals. But I continue to torment my parents about the fact that when my brother graduated, (they were at the end of their working term), and they flew back to America with him and one of their stops was Italy! He bought leather stuff. My sister and I took a redeye flight with a stopover in Nigeria to gas up the plane. It was announced that we could exit the plane if we wanted to, and to be back in about 30 minutes. I told my sister to "Come on, we're gonna get some ivory!" We had to walk past African soldiers with machine guns. They guarded the doorway of the airplane and lined the walk all the way to the terminal - but I got my ivory! My sister wasn't as happy about it as I. She just wanted to be back in the comfort of the airplane. So, I still believe my parents owe me a trip to Italy!

I was having a hard time in adjusting to the States, so I returned to Nairobi to be with Mom and Dad for awhile. I was in Nairobi when my grandpa passed away and when my grandma came to Kenya. I had so much fun when Grams and I went into Nairobi to hang out. We both loved to read, and we loved to visit a certain bookstore where we could buy and trade books. We walked all over Nairobi to window shop and go to the outdoor market. We bought woven baskets of all sizes and shapes. We also bought a lot of wood carvings that were hand carved by the talented Africans. Grams wasn't as tall as I, and she would go home and tell Mom and Dad that she had a hard time keeping up with me and my "long ol' legs." I really enjoyed my time getting to know my grandmother so well – even when she crunched her chips so loudly when I tried to read my books!

There was a restaurant in Nairobi called the Carnivore. It was an open-air restaurant with a large cooking pit in the center.

The tables and chairs were made of large slabs of thick wood. The menu consisted of every kind of game meat available in Kenya! They skewered the meat on large Maasai swords and cooked it on coals. The gazelle was very tender, but the giraffe was quite tough. I chose to not order the zebra - since that's my favorite animal! I'm sure it would have been tough as well. For dessert, we always ordered the ice cream with lychee. The lychee looked like a large skinned grape with the same texture and consistency. It sure tasted a lot better when I realized a "lychee" was a fruit and not a parasite!

We took Grams to the Carnivore. We sat in one of the seating areas which were enclosed by windows. When the windows were open, the cool breeze gently blew in - giving a comfortable outdoor effect, as the restaurant was surrounded by the beautiful African plant life. Mom always made sure to be proper and use etiquette, so we wouldn't get confused with stereotyped savage missionaries. As we talked, she stirred sugar into her hot tea and took a sip. She noticed a piece of tea leaf in her tea, so she quietly took her spoon to scoop it up. Then as lady-like as she could muster, she did a quick flip of the spoon towards the window. She did not realize that the windows were not open that day. The whole spoonful of tea hit the window with a very obvious splat! It was one of those moments when the slightest absurdity leaves one in total hysterics! We all felt that moment as we lost all dignity in our abrupt burst of laughter! After this episode we could not seem to compose ourselves for the rest of the meal.

As we prepared to leave, Grams stood and pushed her chair back not knowing that the table behind us was so close. Her chair pushed into the chair behind her which held a small child. The abrupt force of the chair thrust the small child against the table in which he sat, causing him to immediately explode into an earth-shaking scream as he waved his arms above him! I think Grams almost fell over with a heart attack, while I tried to keep my bladder intact! We apologized over and over as we tried to comfort the child - to no avail. The looks from the parents told us to turn and run! When we turned to find Mom and Dad, they were half-way across the restaurant, and they seemed to not hear us when we called out to them. I might be wrong, but one might assume that they did not want to know us at that particular time! Grams and I were on our own! Fortunately we made it out of the restaurant unscathed! We laughed all the way home! I think Grams had more fun than she ever could have imagined during her stay in Kenya!

I took a trip with a Chinese girlfriend to the Masai Mara - a game reserve somewhere in the middle of Kenya. We flew there in a six passenger plane. We stayed in a hut with a thatched roof. All the huts had animal names. We stayed in the Aardvark. We were there for three nights. It was amazing! At night all the guests sat around a large bonfire while the guide told stories. He told us to not make any movement when a whole herd of zebra walked right beside us! I could have touched them! Of course I didn't try since I did not want to experience a stampede. From my bed, I looked out the window (there was no glass) just in time to see a baby zebra walk right by! We weren't fortunate enough to witness a kill, but did see the remains of a few.

As I walked through the camp one afternoon, I spotted a wild boar. Those animals are very difficult to get a picture of because they are so fast. In my excitement I aimed my camera and slowly stalked that wild animal. After a few steps I remembered they can switch ends quicker than lightening - then I would be the one being stalked! I quietly and carefully stopped and let him run ahead. My dad used to hunt them in Ethiopia, and he told me how dangerous they are. But, like my dad - you do what you can to get the shot! He got some awesome close up shots of giraffes, before he learned that they have a deathly kick! His angels were watching over him.

Kenya will always have a piece of my heart, and I will always partially think of it as home. When I was there we had our fears and there were dangerous aspects, but we tried to be aware and make proper choices of where and when to go to certain places. It certainly wasn't boring and added excitement to life! We were always very cautious, and tried to know the thieves' different schemes and be very aware of everyone. Now in America, I get teased for my overly cautious habits and my conspiracy theories. However, I wasn't aware of the American schemes, so I have learned a lot the hard way.

I had a hard time adjusting to America. It was a different way of life for me - as Africa would be for someone who grew up all their lives in America. But I am very, very proud to be an American and to have some sense of belonging here since it's where my roots are. I cannot keep dry eyes when the National Anthem is sung, and I will always cross my heart and stand for the pledge of allegiance. I cry when our soldiers and veterans stand to be honored for their service to our country, and I am very proud to say that my son is a United States Marine! I am thankful for the opportunity to see other countries and learn about other cultures and Kenya will always be in my blood, but I will always be a proud American!

PLEASE pray for missionary kids and their struggles to find their place in life while their parents are trying to be obedient to their work for the Lord. Some have not been as fortunate as I in their search for "normalcy."

About the Author

LaMoin was reared in a non-Christian family and accepted Christ in a revival meeting in Flint, Michigan. She surrendered her life to the Lord three months after she was saved, and one year later enrolled in Bible college to prepare for whatever the Lord wanted her to do. In college, she met and married Bill Cunningham. They have three adult children and five grandchildren.

She and Bill have been missionaries for 50 years. They have served the Lord in Ethiopia, Kenya, Australia, Romania, Germany, Azores, Hong Kong, and are presently doing mission work in Bali, Indonesia.

She has written two previous books, *Oh, Lord, What Have I Gotten Myself Into?* and *Glad I Didn't Know.* She is very transparent as she permits people to look into the window of her heart to see a "real" person. She admits that she does not always fit the stereotyped image of a missionary. Her goal in opening her heart is to glorify God and to be an encouragement to others to remain faithful to Him. She wants the readers to know that missionaries are real people with all the emotions, temptations, strengths, and weaknesses of any other Christians. Missionaries are not immune to family problems. They experience illnesses and tragedies. They make mistakes. But they are also people who love God and, through many heartaches and difficulties, they press toward the mark for the prize of the high calling of God in Christ Jesus.

LaMoin has much experience in public speaking, and because visa restrictions prevent the Cunninghams from living in Bali full time, she would welcome the opportunity to speak at ladies events during the times that she is in America. You can contact her at: LaMoinBill@aol.com.

FOR ADDITIONAL COPIES CONTACT

LaMoin Cunningham
P.O. Box 804
Talbott, TN 37877

Phone: 423-586-0504
Email: LaMoinBill@aol.com

Website: WWW.LifeWithLaMoin.com